HOW TO FORM
1,200 BARRE CHORDS
YOURSELF FOR
GUITARISTS WHO
CAN READ SHEET MUSIC

Günter Beyer

HOW TO FORM 1,200 BARRE CHORDS YOURSELF FOR GUITARISTS WHO CAN READ SHEET MUSIC

The original edition was published in 2023/2024 by
tredition, Ahrensburg, Germany, under the title:
*1200 BARREGRIFFE SELBST BILDEN FÜR
GITARRISTEN, DIE NOTEN LESEN KÖNNEN*
Translated from the German by Günter Beyer

 **tredition**

© 2023 Günter Beyer, Provinzialstr. 89, DE-66663 Merzig, Germany
e-mail: guenter.beyer3@web.de

ISBN 978-3-384-46855-0

Printing and distribution on behalf of the author:

tredition GmbH, An der Strusbek 10, DE-22926 Ahrensburg, Germany

Contents

I. Preface

I was born in 1941, am self-taught and have never had any guitar or keyboard lessons. In 1962 and 1963 I played dance music in Merzig, Saarland, Germany, in the first band with electric guitars in the following line-up: bass, rhythm and solo guitar, piano and drums. I mainly played rhythm guitar, but also several solo guitar pieces.

Back then we mainly played instrumental music as the "Rag Boys".

Over the next few years, I helped out a few times as a guitarist in other dance bands.

From 2002 I played rhythm guitar with the "Seffersbachlärchen" in Brotdorf, then with the "Funkentöter" (English: spark killers), the fire department choir in Merzig-Brotdorf.

In between, I also played with the Loreley brass band in 2016 and 2017, again in Merzig-Brotdorf. For the medley "James Last Golden Hits", for example, **35** different chords had to be mastered, mainly in B keys.

I would like to take this opportunity to thank my son Sven for valuable tips for the translation in the English and my Persian friend Masoud Shaloo, who quickly introduced me to the Powerpoint program so that I could visualize the many chord patterns, which I was unfortunately unable to do with Excel.

I had already figured out the "barré chord" system very early on. But it was only when I had the idea of representing the fingering points of the simple major chord using different symbols - root = **O**, third = • - and fifth = **Q** (in **German fifth = Q**uinte)- that I was able to offer a good way for any guitarist who can read sheet music to easily understand the system. Changes to the simple major chord are all clearly marked by **larger** signs, **larger** numbers or the **larger** letter **m** for minor in **grey** or **bold black**. In the books available for purchase and on the Internet, the barré fingerings are usually shown in tables as follows:

1. Vertical or horizontal tables with black lines for the 6 guitar strings and the frets as well as black dots.

2. The barré finger is listed as a more or less thick horizontal or vertical line in the table.

3. The 3 grip points of the other fingers are uniformly black and do not differ from each other.

4. It is not clear which chord pattern is used and where the changes in the fingering points are compared to the normal, simple major chord.

5. For each chord C, C sharp, D, D sharp etc. all chord possibilities are listed again.

I list 34+2 chords in C and F. The displacements for C sharp, D, D sharp and from F to F sharp etc. are explained logically, so that all the tables for the possible chords for C sharp, D, D sharp and F sharp, G etc. become redundant.

I believe that you can easily form and find most of the handles yourself. That's why I've created this little work to offer an understandable solution.

The prerequisite is that the player can read a little music, namely App. 1, and also understands it. Being able to play a keyboard instrument makes it even easier to understand.

Please read the preface and the text up to page 47 before studying App. 11 to 15. This is the only way to understand the relationships between the individual barré chords.

My DINA5 booklet contains **34** + 2 (see page 41, point VIII, **C11** and **Cmin11**) = **36** different **C chords** in barré for the guitar, but there are even more.

The explained shifts result in a total of 36 x 12 = **432** different chords from C to B (= 12 semitone steps). As there are usually **up to 3** usable fingering possibilities for a particular chord, which are not too high on the guitar neck, this also means **up to** 432 x 3 = **1,296** chord patterns for chords across all strings - possibly with muted strings.

Another calculation for usable chords: appendices 11 to 15 contain 43+32+22+26+32+2 (see page 41, point VIII.) = a total of **157** chords. If you multiply this number by the possible **12** semitone steps from C to B of an octave, then there are **1,884** different chords. Assuming that approx. **33%** of these are too high on the fingerboard, this results in an average of up to **1,262** playable chords.

In my opinion, this book is a **world first** and therefore a **"must"** for all guitarists who play barré chords.

II. Introduction to the new system

The following abbreviations are used:

App. = **App**endix or **App**endices
CP = **c**hord **p**attern e.g. for the simple major chords without derivatives
m = **m**in or minor tone, ♭3 or **minor** third
I to **XIII** = Roman numerals for frets 1 to 13
IF, M, R and **L** = abbreviation for **i**ndex, **m**iddle, **r**ing and **l**ittle finger
1 to **13** = Arabic numerals for chord tones in scales

Fret numbers in italics means that the barre finger has been moved one or two trets up or down.

By the way, nobody has to reproduce all chord patterns immediately, it is usually enough to know at least 3 variants so that you are prepared for all cases in practice.

II.1 Explanation of the chord pattern C6add9

This chord is also illustrated on the cover. Vertical, slightly thicker lines between fingering points indicate the barré finger(s).

In contrast to other books on barré chords, the "tables" in my book are shown horizontally. The line for the low E string is dotted and lies at the bottom, just as the guitarist sees the strings of his guitar. A fingering diagram only includes 5 frets, 4 for the fingering points and one fret to explain the possible new note by clearly marked **larger** signs, numbers or the letter **m** note in **grey or bold black** for the minor tone.

The chord patterns can therefore be displayed **larger**, as only 5 frets are required for a chord and not 10.

The chord patterns are **sorted according to chord patterns** and arranged starting with the changes on the high E string. The same chords of the different chord patterns are therefore **not next to each other**, but see instead:

Appendix 5	5+1 chord patterns of the **simple major chord**,
Appendix 7	11 chord patterns of the **C7 chord**,
Appendix 8	5 chord patterns of the **simple minor chord**,
Appendix 9	5 chord patterns of the **C7♭9 chord**,
Point IV.3.	E♭Δ7 **chord**, see page 23,
Point VII.5.	E♭m6/Fm6/Cm7♭5/Dm7♭5 **chords**, see page 39, point 5.

The number of the fret for the barré finger in Roman numerals, the name of the chord and the number of the chord pattern are in the first line of the head image; in the second line, there is the abbreviation for the **large** barré finger and any other barré fingers. To the left of the chord pattern, there is the number of the figure pattern and to the right the abbreviation for the other (barré) fingers to be used (**L** for little finger etc.).

The root tone/octave of the simple major chord is shown in black as a round circle (**O**), the third as a thick, black dot (●) and the fifth as a black Q (**Q**), in German **Q**uinte, so that all three possible notes of the simple major chord are covered. A dampened string is marked with a black X (**X**).

The designation as a third or fifth is always **based** on a **lower** - sometimes **fictitious – root note**.

In the case of changes to the simple major chord, the signs and letters are all shown in clearly marked **larger** numbers or/and the letter **m** in **grey or bold black** to the right of the new fingering point.

To illustrate this, here is an example of the C6add9 chord according to chord pattern **1,** which is also shown on the cover.

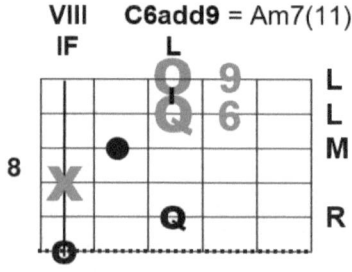

Fingering for chords

IF = index finger
M = middle finger
R = ring finger
L = little finger
Grip points connected
with vertical line(s)
= barre finger(s)

The little finger on the **B string** in the 10th fret is bent and can therefore play the **6th** and **9th** notes of the Cmajor scale. The letter **L** in the 2nd line in the head and the connecting line between the two **large** fingering points in **grey or bold black** indicate the little finger as the 2nd barré finger. The finger on he 8th fret of the D string has been raised slightly and is now damped with the big barré finger, hence the **large X** in **grey or bold black**. Apart from the index finger as the barré finger, there are normally only 3 fingers available for the other fingering points.

Below you can see the simple Cmajor chord with the fingering points root, third and fifth. If the fingering point on the high E string with the note **8 is designated** as **C** of the Cmajor scale, then the designations a **9th** note for **D** on the high E string 2 frets higher and also on the B string 2 frets higher the **6th** note for **A** are quite logical.

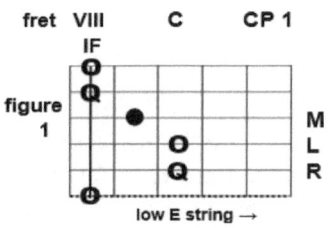
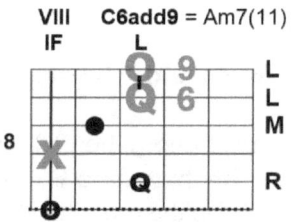

In my case, the position of a note, whether in the 1st, 2nd or 3rd octave, is irrelevant; the notes are given without additional numbers for the octaves, which serves to simplify the representation and for later shifts.

The higher the string on which the new note of an altered chord is struck, the better and clearer it sounds. Example: **C6** with chord pattern 2, 1st barré finger on fret III, the little finger on fret V over the strings D, G, B and E serves as the 2nd barré finger. The note **A** sounds on the high E string in fret V, see also App. 12, figure 6.

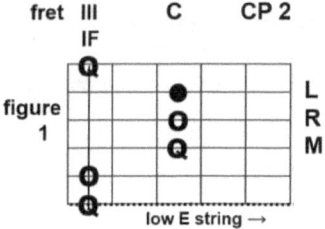
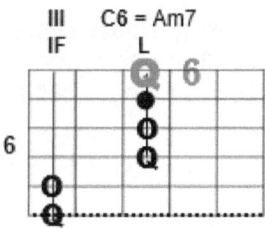

If the newly added note is heard several times in different octaves, the new chord is clearly distinct from the original chord, example: **Fm**, developed from the Fmajor chord, App. 13, chord pattern 3, figure 2. The note **A flat** is present **3 times** here, see also page 20, explanations to the App. 13, fig. 2.

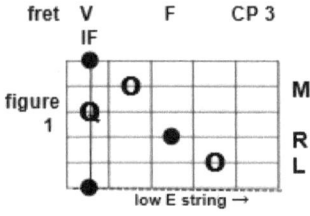

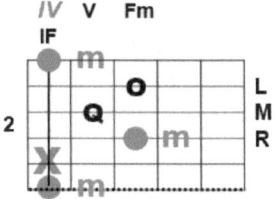

II.2 Structure of major chords

The simple major chord, here **C**, consists of only 3 different tones, the **root**, here **C** (= **O**), the third, here **E** (= •) and the fifth, here **G** (= **Q**). The third is 4 semitones above the root, the fifth 7 semitones above the root. As the guitar has 6 strings, some notes are represented two or three times, which is irrelevant. **The order of the notes is also irrelevant**. But **each note** must occur **at least once**, even in later derivations.

I call the **7th** note of the Cmajor scale **B, which is** usually listed as H in Germany. I call the next note, lowered by half a tone, **B♭**, known as B in Germany.

A special feature of the chord name here is that C7 is not the seventh note of the Cmajor scale: C7 does not mean that the seventh note of the Cmajor scale is added, but the note **B♭,** which is 2 semitones lower than the root note. With chord **C7maj** only the 7th note of the Cmajor scale, namely **B**, is added to the simple Cmajor chord.

C7 and CΔ7 are possible chords, otherwise the notes correspond to the number in App. **3** in one or more octaves. The chord **D7** therefore consists of the notes D, F♯, A and 2 half notes below the octave of the root note **C**.

In an Add9 chord, the 9th note can also be on the low E string, example: appendix 14, figures 9 and 11, as we will learn later.

The simple **Cm** chord consists of the 3 notes C, E♭ and G.

II.3 Designation of the chords

I designate all chords with the necessary numbers and letters, there is no **Csus** for me, the chord is either **Csus2** or Csus4, just as **C9** only corresponds to the chord **Cadd9** for me and not **C7add9**, as is often stated. I can only understand the new chord and reproduce it myself if all the changes compared to the simple Cmajor chord are listed exactly in numbers and/or letters.

Here are examples of simple major chords and the notes:

Cmajor = tones C+E+G   Gmajor = tones G+B+D
Dmajor = tones D+F♯+A   Amajor = tones A+C♯+E
Emajor = tones E+G♯+B   Bmajor = tones B+D♯+F♯
Fmajor = tones F+A+C

D♭major = D♭+F+A♭   A♭major = A♭+C+E♭

E♭major = E♭+G+B♭   B♭major = B♭+D+F

G♭major = G♭+B♭+D♭

For cross key, we have:

C sharp chord = C♯ = **Cis chord** = tones C♯ + E♯ (=F) + G♯ and so on.

If you know the notes of the simple major chords for all keys by heart and can reliably determine their position on the individual strings for the simple major chords, it will not be difficult for you to understand and reproduce all derivations later on. Otherwise, realize again that the third is 4 semitones above the root, the fifth 7 semitones above the - sometimes **fictitious** - root.

Difference between Cadd9 and Csus2

The **Cadd9 chord consists** of the **4** notes C, E, G and **D** in a different octave. The **Csus2** chord only consists of the **3 notes** C, D and G, the note **E** is missing!

II.4 The 5+1 Chords with empty strings and the CP

With empty strings you can play the 5 chords **C, D, E, G** and **A** on the first **3** frets of the guitar as so-called open chords, the G chord even in 2 variations.

This means that every major chord can be played as a barré chord in 5 variations, with the 2nd variation of chord pattern 5, even in 6, by replacing the nut with the barré finger and sliding it upwards on the guitar neck (see appendices 5 and 6). Sometimes you would have to move too far up, so that some chords above the 10th fret are not normally played, but they are there.

I have numbered the **chord patterns** (**CP**) according to popularity.

CP **1** = developed from **E** string open chord over frets 1 – 3,
CP **2** = developed from **A** string open chord over frets 1 – 3,
CP **3** = developed from **C** string open chord over frets 1 – **4,**
CP **4** = developed from **D** string open chord over frets 1 – **4,**
CP **5** = developed from **G** string open chord over frets 1 – **4**.

It is important to remember this order because it is maintained throughout the booklet, see appendices 5 and 6. I refer to altered major chords as derivations.

Chord patterns 1 and 2 are easier to grip because they usually only extend over 3 frets.

You should memorize the designation of the individual notes as root, third or fifth for all major chords, as they are marked differently as a circle (**O=root**), thick dot (●=third) or Q (**Q = fifth**). This is to remember the derivations more easily as we will see later.

II.5 Derivations of major chords

The number(s) after the root note of a major or minor chord indicate one or more new notes in the chord. The **large** letter **m** in **grey or bold black** stands for a minor chord.

C6, for example, means that the new note **A** is added to the simple major chord C as the **6th** note of the Cmajor scale, i.e. the new note **A** is added to the notes C, E and G.

The chords **C7(6)** and derivatives thereof should actually be called **C7(13)** etc., because in a chord the seventh and the 6th note of a scale never occur in the same octave, the sound would be as bad as a shrill fire engine siren. In addition, there is normally no barré fingering over 6 strings. However, the notation 7(6) makes it easier to classify the new notes correctly, because the **13th** note of the Cmajor scale is not directly known as "**A**".

We differentiate between the derivations of major chords:

1. Chords with newly added notes such as **C6**, **C7**, **CΔ7**, **Cb9**, **C9** as well as **C7(6)**, **C7add9**, **C7b9**, **C7add9(13)** etc.

2. Chords in which the new notes displace other notes such as **Csus2** (D displaces E), **Cm** (Eb displaces E), **Csus4** (F displaces E), **Caug** (G♯ displaces G) and **Cverm7**, in which all notes except the root are lowered by half a tone (**Eb** displaces E, **Gb** displaces G and **A** displaces Bb) and

3. Mixed forms of 1 and 2 such as **C7sus4** (notes C, **F,** G and **Bb**, the note **E** is missing), as well as **C7b5, C7♯5** without the tone **G.**

II.6 Chords with 2 or more root notes

In App. 11 to 15, the names of other chords with other root notes are also listed, but not in bold. The tones of the chords are listed from bottom to top:

Csus2 = Gsus4 = C+D+G = G+C+D
Csus4 = Fsus2 = C+F+G = F+G+C
Caug = Eaug = G♯aug = C+E+G♯ = E+G♯+C = G♯+C+E
C6 = Am7 = C+E+G+A = A+C+E+G
C6add9 = Am7(11) = Am7/4 = C+E+G+A+D = A+C+E+G+D
Cverm7 = Ebverm7 = Gbverm7 = Averm7 = C+Eb+Gb+A
Cm7b5 = Ebm6 = C+Eb+Gb+Bb = Eb+Gb+Bb+C

III. Notes on the appendices

III.1 App. 1 C chords in notes

The chords are shown here in notes, starting with the three notes, the root **C,** the third **E** and the fifth **G** for the simple **Cmajor chord**. The classification as a third or fifth is always based on a lower, sometimes **fictitious, root note.** Also, the European expressions are mentioned, also in App. 2.

However, the guitar has 6 strings, so some notes actually occur up to three times, but this is irrelevant for further understanding. A distinction for the individual octaves is also not required.

As you can see from bar 2 - **Csus2** - from the new notes as **large** black dots, the 2nd note of the new Cmajor chord ascends from **D** in semitone steps upwards from **Csus2** to **Cadd9** (**D** an octave higher).

It should not be confusing if, for example, the 9th note also appears on the low E string in later chord patterns. It is only important that all the notes shown appear at least once in the chord pattern. Examples: appendix 14, figures 9, 11, 15, 17, 19, 21 and 25.

The minor chords are not specifically listed except for the single minor chord but see appendix 2, where they can be found explicitly.

III.2 App. 2 C chords in letters and numbers

In this appendix, all the required notes of a chord are listed in the last right-hand column according to the abbreviated notation for guitar chords, with letters in **grey or bold black** indicating changes compared to the simple Cmajor chord.

The tone sequences begin with the root note and represent the ideal in order to **increase understanding. In reality the sequence is quite different,** the root note is rarely the first note on the guitar except for chord patterns 1 and 5. The double notes have also been omitted. All minor chords are listed here.

I have only used the correct spelling with superscript numbers and letters here. In the rest of the text this has been omitted for the sake of simplicity and because in the text with chord indications the corresponding line spacing would then always have had to be increased in height, for example $C^{7/9}$. In Germany plus or minus chords are often marked with + or -, unlike abroad, for example: **C7/9 minus** = C7♭9 or **C7/5+** = C7#5 abroad.

III.3 App. 3 Piano keyboard for C and F chords

Here we see the notes of the simple **C** and **F** major chord above the bold outlined numbers.on the piano keyboard. The numbers from 2 to 13 show the possible new tones and thus new chords/derivations.

III.4 App. 4 Guitar neck with all notes

Here are all the notes on the guitar neck but shown as # keys. The boldly outlined frets are the frets that are normally marked with a dot or wide bands of mother-of-pearl. Fret XII indicates the 1st octave on the E strings; the octave in question has not been indicated.

For solos from the 13th fret onwards, the notes are the same as on frets I to VIII, but a whole octave higher.

III.5 App. 5 5+1 CP of the simple major chord

The 5+1 chord patterns with fingering and symbols for the root/octave (O), the third (●) and the fifth (Q) are shown here. The fret indication on the guitar neck has been omitted because the chord pattern does not change regardless of where you finger the chord. The order of the chord patterns depends on the popularity of the fingerings. It always remains the same throughout the text, so please remember it!

III.6 App. 6 5+1 CP of the Fmajor chord

Here are the 5+1 possible chord patterns for the simple **F chord**, fret **I**, as well as for all other basic notes from fret I to fret X for the barré finger in ascending order on the guitar neck.

III.7 App. 7 11 Fingering pattern of the C7 chord

Here are 11 possibilities for seventh chords, the 5 underlined in **grey or bold black** are particularly easy to finger. Chord pattern 1 is particularly recommended! It was a tip from our German teacher Mr. Kelkel from Gymnasium Am Stefansberg in Merzig in 1961.

However, there are other possibilities for seventh chords, as can be seen in App. 15, figures 10 and 13. In my opinion, the chord patterns are probably quite uncommon.

III.8 App. 8 Fingering pattern of the minor chord

The 3 recommended and easily accessible options are also underlined in **grey or bold black**.

III.9 App. 9 5 Fingering pattern of the C7♭9 chord

Fingering pattern 1 for C7♭9 can be explained simply as follows: Fingering on the 8th fret with chord pattern 1 the simple Cmajor chord, go down 2 half notes with the barré finger to fret **VI** and then finger the corresponding **dim7** chord, in this case the **B♭verm7 chord**, and from bottom to top you have the notes **B♭, E, B♭, D♭, G** and **B♭** again, all notes that belong to the chord **C7♭9**. If you now move your little finger from the B♭ string back to the high **E** string, you will produce the missing **root note C**, so that all the necessary notes of the **C7♭9** chord are now present.

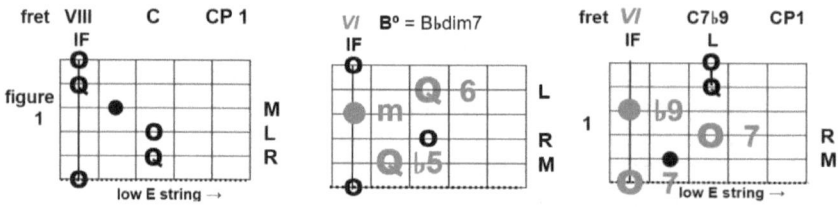

I almost think that the fingering of this new derivation was mostly unknown until now, because it is not listed on the Internet under "all guitar chords".

Fingering pattern 3 is easy to memorize, as according to chord pattern **1** for the simple Cmajor chord, the barré finger is only moved one fret higher, the fingers on the **A** and **D** strings are not moved higher. The little finger for fingering the third is freed up by the advanced barré finger; the new fingering with the note **B♭** is shown in figure 3.

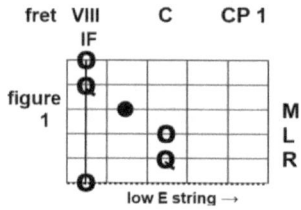
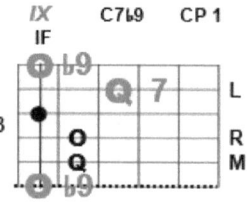

Fingering pattern 5 was created from App. 12, figure 13, by moving the barré finger one fret higher, the other fingers remain in their old positions. The raised barré finger produces the ♭9 note **D♭** on the A string, while the note A♭ would be produced on the low E string, but this does not match the C7♭9 chord and must therefore be muted or must not be struck.

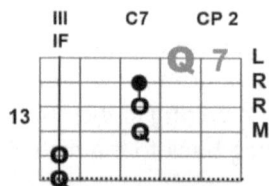
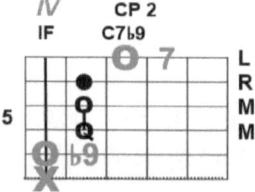

III.10 App. 10 Chords with muted strings

As there are only **3 other** fingers available for the various fingering patterns in addition to the barré finger, one or more strings have to be muted from time to time, as the guitar has 6 strings and only 4 fingers can usually be used.

In the examples shown here, the new chords are also listed if the damping is removed, or a neighboring string is accidentally damped or not damped. Completely different chords with different root tones can be created, see figures 10 and 11. Figures 25 and 26, for example, differ only in that in figure 26 the barré finger is pressed all the way through so that the seventh on the D string sounds anew and the new chord C7add9(13) = C7add9(6) is created from C6add9, which is very shrill and can only be used as a final chord.

III.11 App. 11 Chord pattern 1 with derivations

Applies to all grip patterns in Appendices **11 to 15** and in part to Appendices **16 to 18**

App. 11, figure 1 shows the simple major chord. In Fig. **1A,** the numbers and the letter m for minor on the individual strings in **grey or bold black** indicate the possible new notes as numbers for altered simple major chords = derivations.

In contrast to the fingering diagrams 2 to the end of the appendices, the **large** numbers and the **large** letter m for **m**inor in **grey or bold black** represent the **exact** fingering point in diagram **1A** on the respective string.

However, in the **large** altered fingerings **2** and following, the numerical number of the newly added note is shown in **grey or bold black** to **the right of** the **large** dot, the **large** circle or the **large Q**, a **large** "m" stands for the **m**inor note.

App. 11, figure 2, **C7♭9 chord**. The numbers ♭9 and **7** are shown to the right of the **large** circles in **grey or bold black,** indicating that the new notes have arisen from the root note or an octave of it; here they are the notes **D flat** and **B♭**.

App. 11, figure 4 is easily explained: Pick CP 1 as shown in Fig. 1, now move the barré finger one fret higher and you have the ♭9 note **D flat** on the E strings. The finger on the G string is now free. The new fingering with the new note of the B string on fret XI is the seventh - here the note **Bb.** See also page 17, point III.9, figures 1 and 3!

<u>Figure 10</u> The final chord C7add9(13) sounds quite hard and weird.

<u>Figures 16 to 18</u> are to be understood in such a way that the fingering chord with the barré finger on the 4th, 8th and 12th frets always produces the **C**aug chord. **C**aug chord. = **E**aug = **G#**aug.

<u>Figures 35 to 38</u> The same applies here. With the barré finger on the second, the fifth, the eighth and the eleventh frets, I create the diminished seventh chord **C°. C° = Eb° = Gb = A°.**

III.12 App. 12 Chord pattern 2 with derivations

<u>Figure 2 (C7add9) and figure 6 (C6)</u> are chords that are easy to finger and sound great at an angle.

<u>In chord patterns 3 to 5,</u> the same chord patterns with the barré finger on frets IV, VIII and XII always lead to the **C**aug chord, **C**aug = **E**aug = **G#**aug.

<u>Figure 14</u> was created from figure 13 by moving the barré finger one fret higher in order to produce the b**9 note D flat** on the **A** string; the low E string has to be muted because the newly produced note G **sharp** no longer fits the chord C7b9.

The chord patterns in appendix 12 are mostly spread over only 3 frets, exceptions: figures 13, 15, 24 to 27 and 29.

<u>Figure 32</u> Here the new chord **Csus2sus4** that is fairly unknown in Germany.

III.13 App. 13 Chord pattern 3 with derivations

The chord patterns usually extend over 4 frets. Derivations of these chords over only 3 frets are more popular and easier to finger.

<u>Figure 2</u> Here the barré finger is placed one fret down towards the nut so that the note **A flat** sounds on the E strings. The other fingers also had to be partially moved, as shown in figure 2. See also page 40, point VII, last row below, figures 1 and 2!

<u>Figure 4</u> is an easy-to-grasp and good-sounding seventh chord, the root note is on the B string, which is important for a shift. The chord can be played over

all 6 strings despite the 2 strings being damped. The fingers on the B string and the low E string should be bent slightly backwards so that the high **E** and **A** strings are damped.

If this chord is memorized, then the derivations of this chord, namely fig. 5 (**F7sus4**) and 6 (**F7♭5**) according to appendix 13, are quite logical.

Figure 26 Here the new chord **Csus2sus4** that is fairly unknown in Germany.

III.14 App. 14 Chord pattern 4 with derivations

It should be noted here that the low E string is usually damped. If this is not the case, the ninth note is added, examples: Fm6 (fig. 10) → Fm6**add9** figure 11), F7 (fig. 16) → F7**add9** (fig. 17).

Figure 26 Here the new chord **Csus2sus4** that is fairly unknown in Germany

III.15 App. 15 Chord pattern 5 with derivations

Figure 11 is worth mentioning here for the **Cmaj7** chord, which also only extends over **3** frets.

Figure 30 Here the new chord **Csus2sus4** that is fairly unknown in Germany. The figures 31 and 32 were added later.

III.16 App. 16 Personal chord fingerings for notation

Here you can note your chord patterns as you wish.

III.17 App. 17 and 18 CP 1 to 5 large with derivations

The chord patterns 1 to 2 (App. 17) and 3 to 5 (App. 18) are shown in **large** size so that the **large** numbers and the **large** letter m (minor) in **grey or bold black** for new notes in the simple major chord are more clearly recognizable, which significantly increases the understanding of new chords/derivations.

IV. Forming a major chord - Displacements

As only **C** and **Fmajor chords** are listed in appendices 11 to 15, it is necessary to make shifts when searching for other chords. Using the examples for the **Amajor chord** and the **E** flat **major chord** in **barré version,** the system of displacements is explained.

IV.1 Forming an Amajor chord in barré version

In CP **1,** the root note **A** is on the **E strings**, i.e. here on the fifth fret, which fits perfectly. The chord only requires 3 frets, is easy to play and sounds good. If you are looking for a derivation of the **A** major chord, continue reading under points **V.** or **VI.**

IV.2 Forming an Eb major chord

You always have to remember which note is on the high E string for each chord pattern.

In chord pattern **1, the root note or 2nd octave is** on the high and low **E string**. Here the barré finger would have to be moved up to fret **XI** for the **Eb chord**, which is normally too high.

In chord pattern **2,** the **fifth is** on the E strings, so for the E flat chord the note **Bb** is on the **6th** fret, which fits perfectly here.

In chord pattern **3,** the **third** is on the **E strings**, i.e. the note **G**, here on the **third** fret, the chord position is fine. However, the chord pattern extends over 4 frets.

In chord pattern **4,** the **third** is also on the high **E-string**, but the barré finger is 2 frets below the finger on the high E-string, the low E string must be muted, otherwise the chord fits, but also goes over 4 frets.

In chord pattern **5,** the note **Eb** is also produced on the two E strings on the **11th** fret as in chord pattern 1. However, the barré finger is 3 frets lower on the **8th** fret. This is not a popular chord pattern; the chord goes over 4 frets and is hardly ever used except perhaps at high pitches as a final chord.

IV.3 Forming an E♭Δ7 chord

Since the fundamental tone occurs at least twice in all 5 chord patterns, the fundamental tone must be lowered by half a tone at least once so that in our case the tone **D** = **Δ7** can be produced.

CP 1 = We play the E♭major chord with the barré finger on fret XI and then the **major** seventh as shown below:

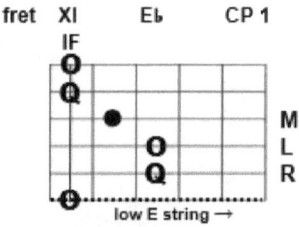 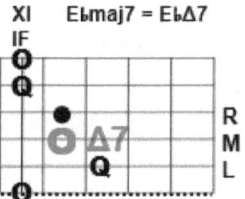

The chord lies too high on the guitar neck and thus fails. For **FΔ7** (first fret) to **CΔ7** (8th fret), however, the fingering is easy to use.

CP 2 = We play the E♭major chord with the barré finger on fret **VI** and then the **major** seventh as shown below:

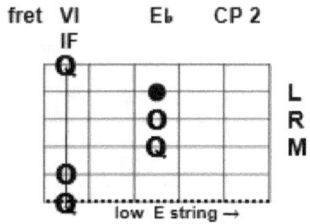 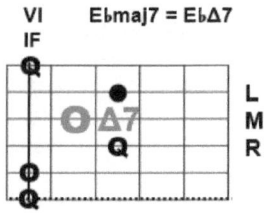

The chord is easy to play and sounds good.

CP 3 = We play the E flat major chord with the barré finger on fret III and then the **major** seventh as shown on the next figure. There are 2 possibilities:

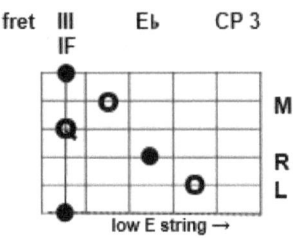

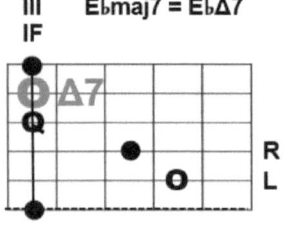

or

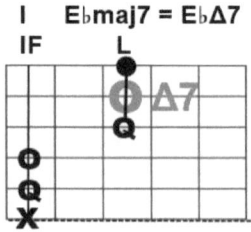

CP 4 = We play the Ebmajor chord with the barré finger on fret I and then the **major** seventh as shown below.

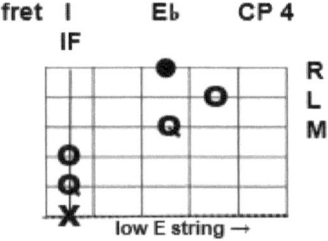

CP 5 = We play the Ebmajor chord with the barré finger on fret VIII and then the **major** seventh as shown below:

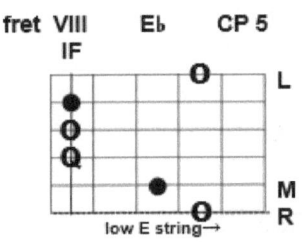

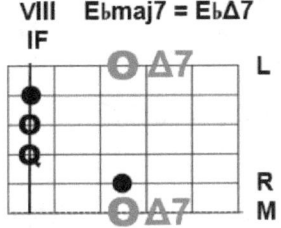

V. Logical changes for new chords/derivations

V.1 Shifts Chord Pattern 1 App. 11 and App. 17

It starts with the simple Cmajor chord, followed by two **C7b9 chords** by sliding a finger or the barré finger forward on the **high** E string, and two **Add9 chords** with a muted D or A string by sliding the finger forward again.

Shifts on the **high E**-string

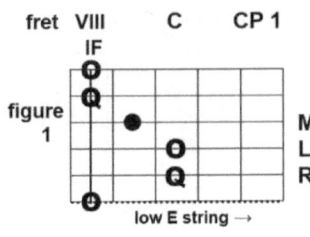

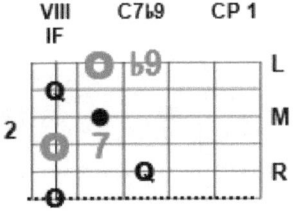

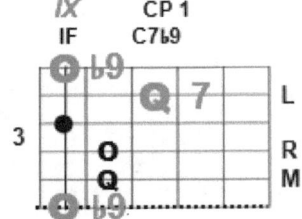

Fingering pattern number 3, on the right, is much easier for me to grasp.

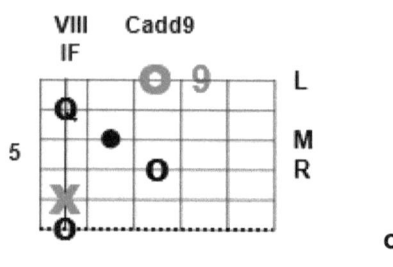

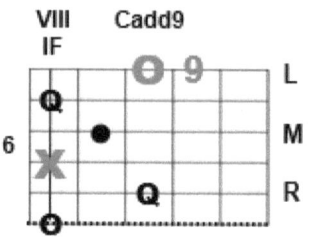

or

Shifts on the **B-string CP 1**

C(major), **Caug, C6**, **C7**

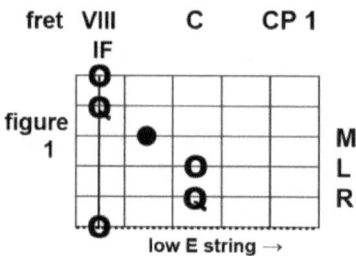

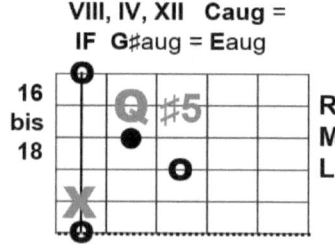

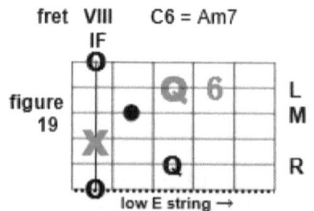

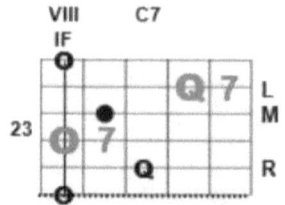

Shifts on the **G** string **CP 1**

Raise middle finger

Cm, C(major)**, Csus4**

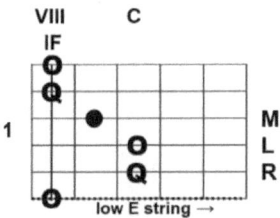

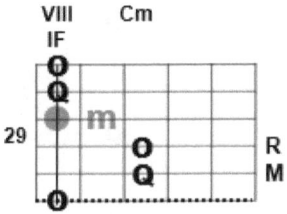

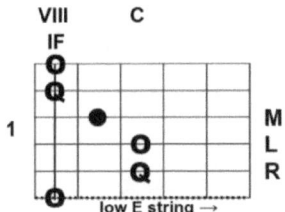

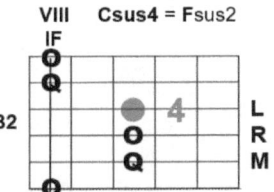

If I now lift my finger on the A-string at figure 32, I have a 2nd fourth.

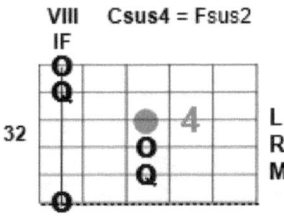

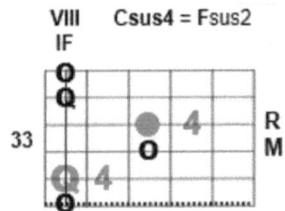

Shifts on the **D** string **CP 1**

Raise little finger

C7, CΔ7, C(major), **Cb9**

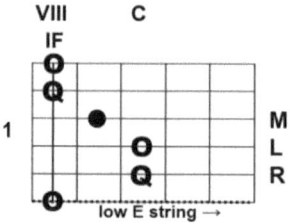

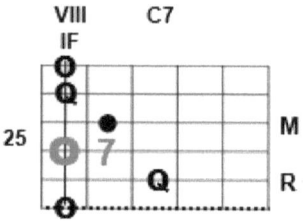

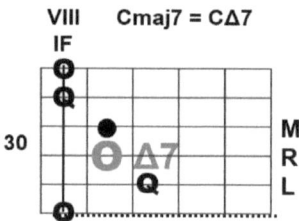

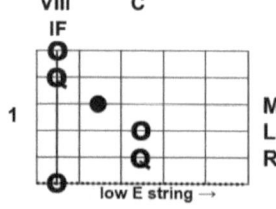

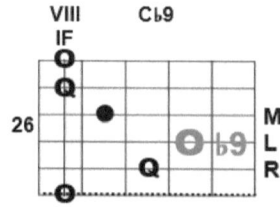

V.2 Shifts Chord Pattern 2 App. 12 and App. 17

on the high E-string CP 2

C(major), Caug, C6, C7

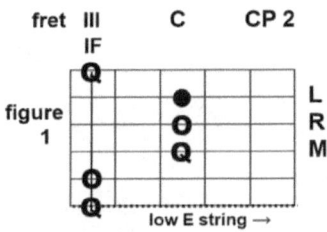

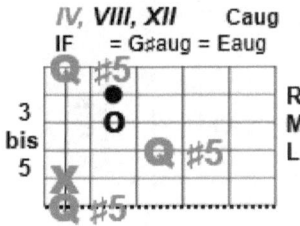

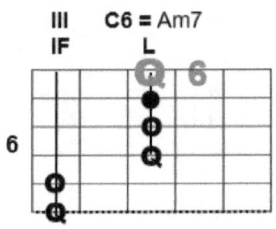

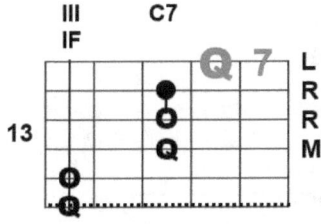

Shifts on the **B s**tring CP **2**

Raise little finger

Csus2, **Cm**, **C**(major), **Csus4**

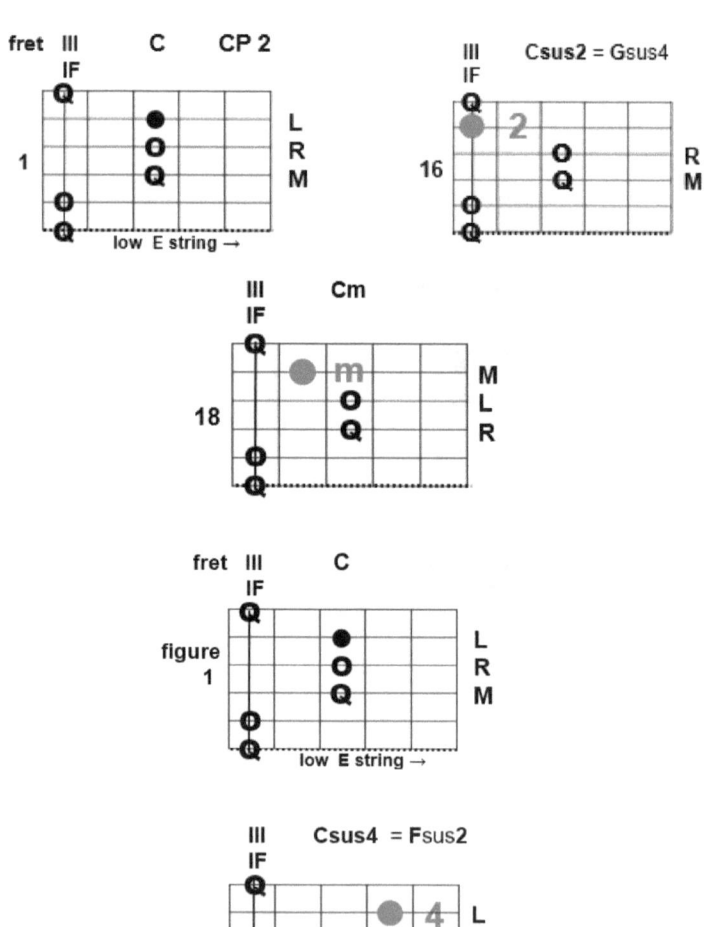

Shifts on the **G** string **CP 2**

Raise ring finger
C7, CΔ7, C, C♭9

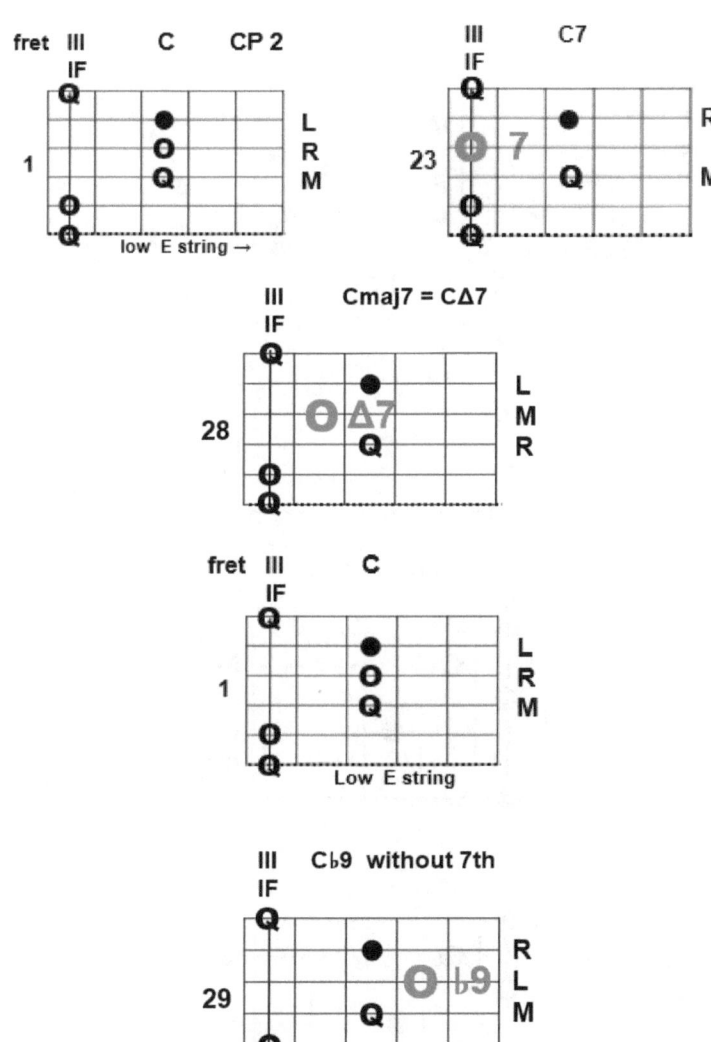

V.3 Shifts Chord Pattern 3 App. 13 and App. 18

lift the little finger
on the **A**-string

F6, **F7**, **FΔ7**, **F**

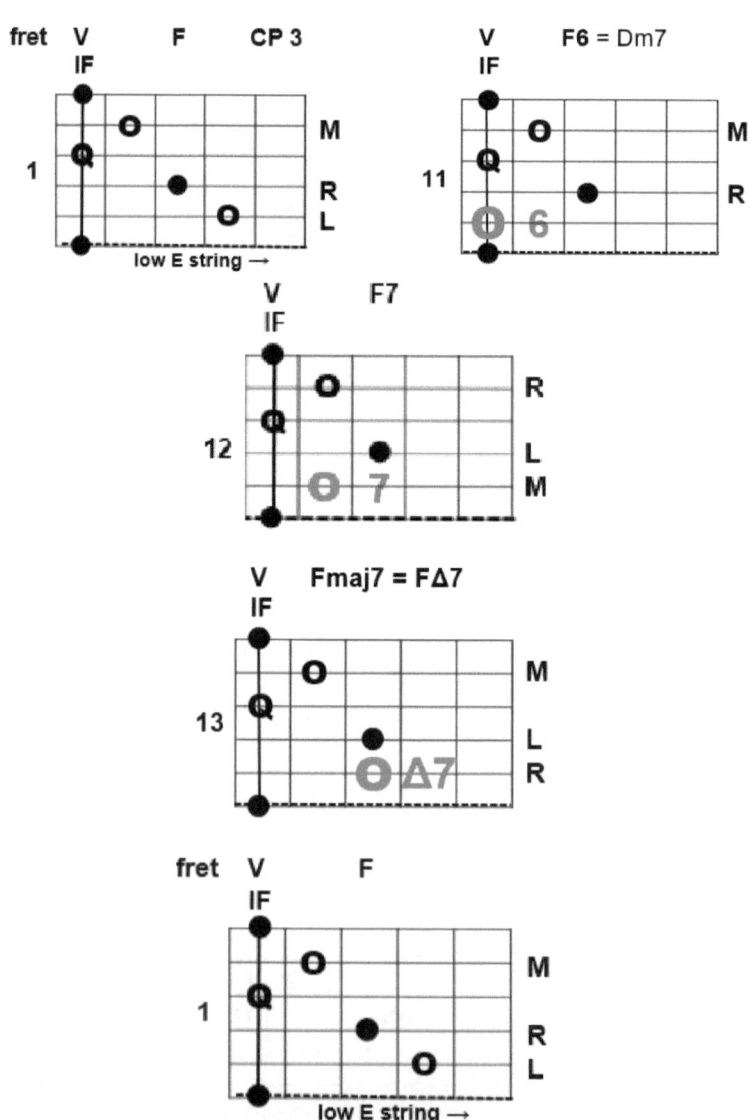

V.4 Shifts Chord Pattern 4 App. 14 and App. 18

on the B string CP 4

Fmaj, FΔ7, F7, F6

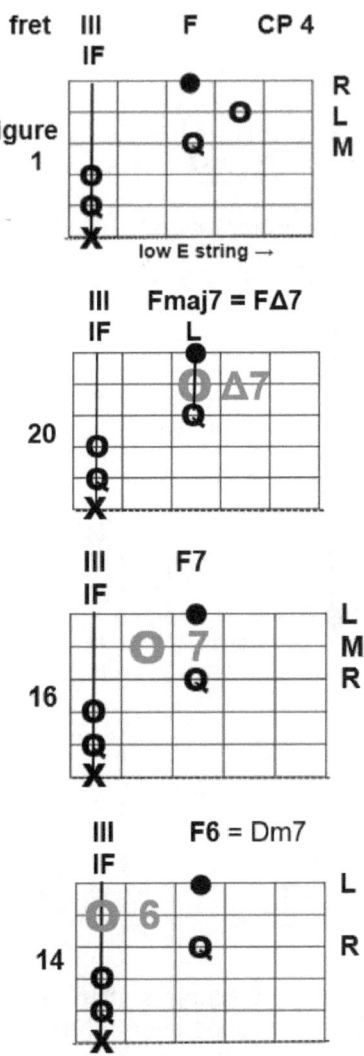

V.5 Shifts Chord Pattern 5, App. 15 and App. 18

on the high **E**-string

Cmaj, **CΔ7**, **C7** and **C6**

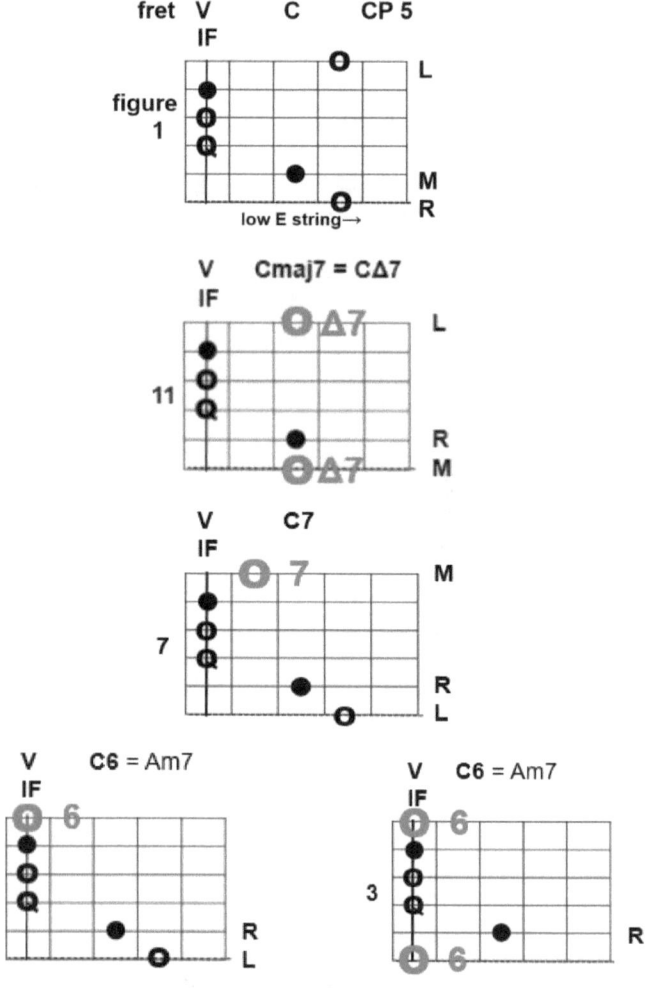

In figure 3, the finger on the low E-string is lifted up, a new sixth has been created, the fingering pattern only goes over 3 frets.

The examples shown for chord patterns 1 to 5 are only an excerpt, but they illustrate well the system of displacements for new chords or derivations.

I believe that once you have consciously found and formed a new chord with a derivation yourself, you won't forget the derivation so quickly. If you know which note you are producing on each string with the simple Cmajor chord, you immediately understand the shift.

VI. Forming an unknown chord

For a quick search - chords are **next to each other**

after simple major **chords** see App. **5,**
after the simple **seventh chord** see App. **7,**
and after the simple **minor chord** see App. **8,**
after **7b9 chords** see App. **9,**
after **maj7 chords** see **page 23 ff, point IV.3,**
after **minor 6 chords** or **m7b5 chords** see also **page 39, point VII, 5.**

Otherwise, to form a new chord, proceed as follows:

Finger the simple **Cmajor** chord at fingering patterns **1, 2** and **5,** finger the simple **Fmajor** chord at fingering patterns **3** and **4**. Then form the **C** or **F** chord again with all the numbers and possibly the letter **m** and after this shift to the chord you are looking for.

1. If it is a **minor chord,** then form the minor third; often only one finger has to be moved one fret towards the nut or one finger raised.

2. If I only want to use chord patterns 1 and 2, because here I only need to finger over 3 frets, I have to remember that with chord pattern **1** the **root note** is on the **E strings**, with chord pattern **2** it is the **fifth**. If I'm looking for an **Eb chord,** only chord pattern **2** with the barré finger on the **6th** fret is a possibility; with chord pattern **1** I would have to move up to the **11th** fret, the chord no longer sounds good and is often difficult to finger so high on guitars without an indentation.

Example **1**: I want to form the chord **C7sus 4** with chord pattern **2**.

1. I finger **C** chord with barré finger on the third fret, App. **12**, figure 1.

2. I form the **C7** chord by lifting the ring finger.

3. I move the little finger on the **B** string half a tone higher from the third from E to **F** and have the chord **C7sus4**.

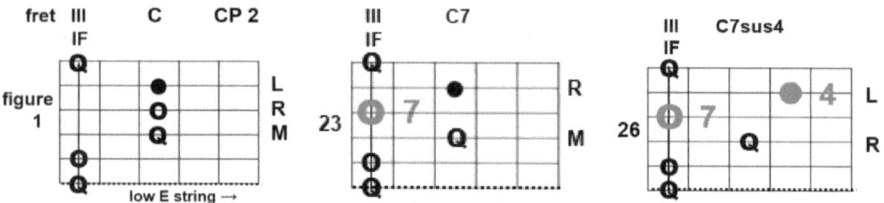

Example 2: I want to form the diminished seventh of C, i.e. **Cº**. As we know, the notes are the root note **C** as well as **E flat, G flat** and **A**.

I play the simple **Cmajor** chord using chord pattern **1**, barré finger on fret **VIII**. I now only have the root note **C**, which corresponds to the chord dim7 I am looking for. The altered notes **E flat, G flat** and **A** are missing.

I finger the **Cm** chord by lifting the middle finger and now producing the note **E flat** again. By the way, the barré finger always remains on the **8**th fret!

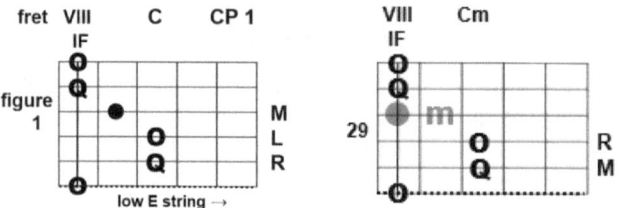

I form the Cm**6** chord. I can place the freed finger for the minor chord on the **B** string 2 frets higher in front of the barré finger, so that the **6th** note of the Cmajor scale, note **A,** is formed, which matches **Cº**.

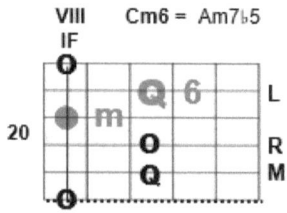

All that is missing now is the note **G flat**, i.e. a fifth lowered by half a tone. The fifth on the A string of the C chord remains unchanged, in this case the note **G**. I can move the finger slightly one fret in the direction of the nut so that the note **G flat** is found.

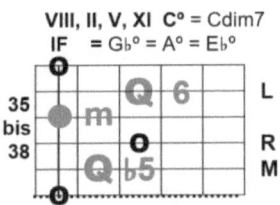

I now have all the notes of the diminished seventh chord of **C**. Since we have memorized the notes of the C° chord - **C+E flat+G flat+A** - we know that I can also play the **C°** chord with the same chord pattern with the barré finger on the **second** fret = G♭° or the **5**th fret = **A°**. The **11**th fret = **E♭°** - would be a little too high, but also correct.

VII. Chords that are difficult to derive

   1.   **C7 chord** according to App. 7, figure 1, and App. 13, figure 4, shown here as **F7** with 2 damped strings.

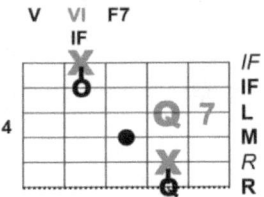

This seventh can easily be shifted from the first fret, C7, to the **8**th fret, G7.

Once you have internalized this grip pattern, the derivations according to App. 13, Figures 5 and 6, are very easy to understand, as they are only logical.

The fingering for the **C7** chord with 2 damped strings is **highly recommended**, as it is very easy to finger and also sounds good. If I have to finger the corresponding tonic to the dominant C7, in this case the Fmajor chord, I can jump to C7 in a flash without leaving fret **I**!

2. Two **C7b9 chords** according to App. 9, fig. 1 and 4, and App. 12, fig. 31

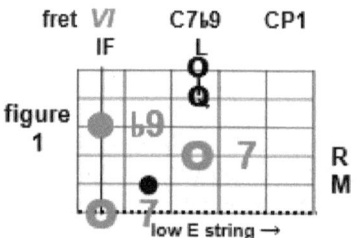
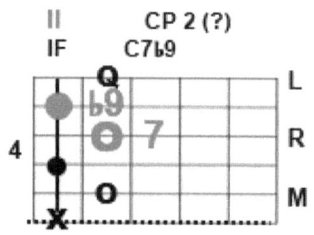

3. The chord **C7add9** App. **12**, figure 2, is also part of this.

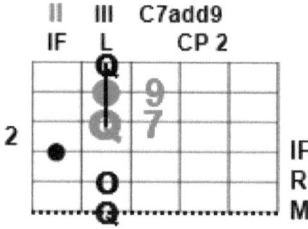

This chord pattern is also easy to play, sounds good and slightly slanted.

4. **C7 chord** according to App. 7, figure 3, and App. 13, figure 14. The chord pattern for this is not clear to me.

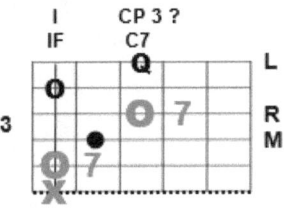

Once this chord is memorized, the derivations according to App. 13, figures 15 to 20 are quite logical.

It is best to memorize these **5** chord fingerings according to points **1** to **4** so that you can now find all the other fingerings except point **4** yourself. Reading the explanations in the appendices under point II. can be a good help.

5. **Cm7b5,** the rare chord name, can only be formed under this name with **CP 1**, see appendix **11** figure **42**. However, if I know the substitute chord with the same notes, there are no problems. **Cdur** becomes **Cm** because **E** is replaced by **E flat**. If I now add the endings **m6** to E flat, I have the substitute chord **Ebm6**, which can very well be derived. There are at least 7 other variants under this name, which are shown below as Cm6 or Fm6.

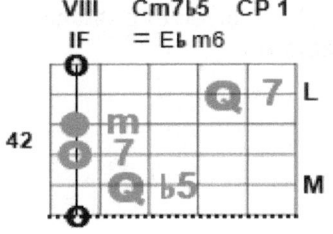
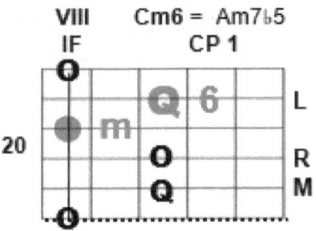

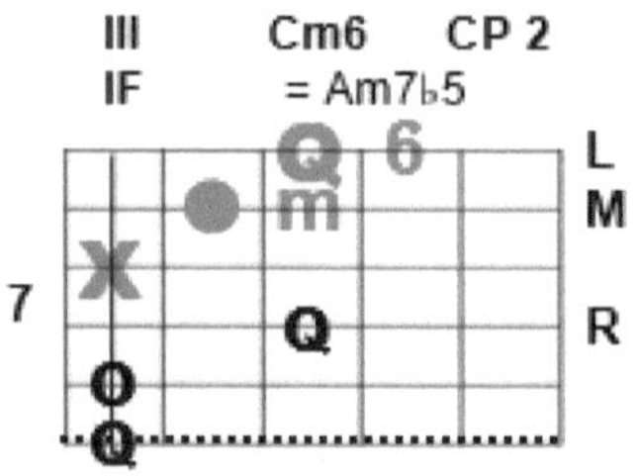

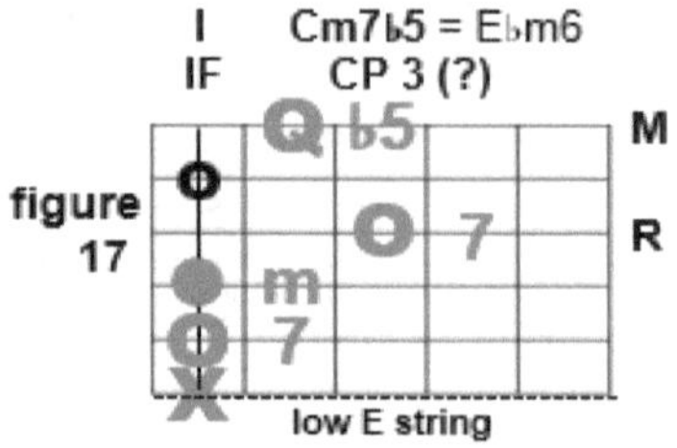

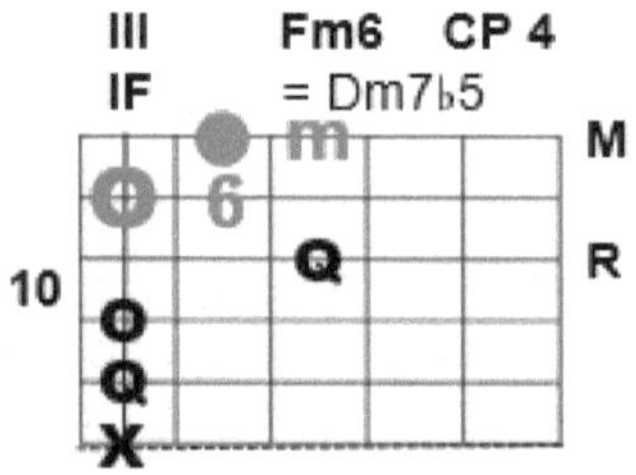

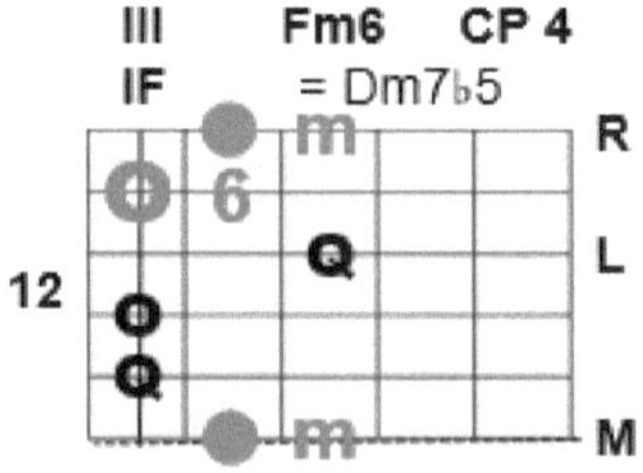

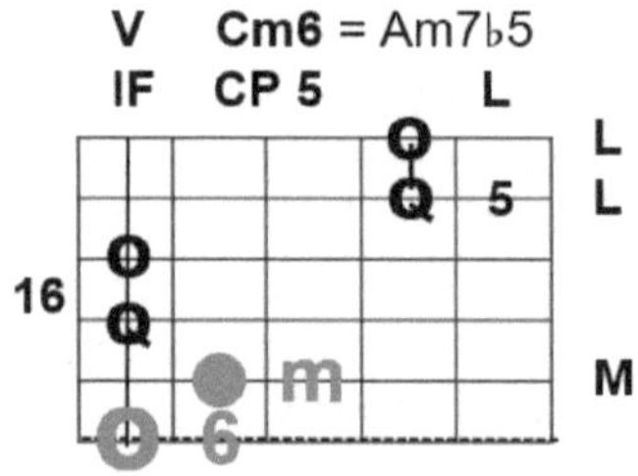

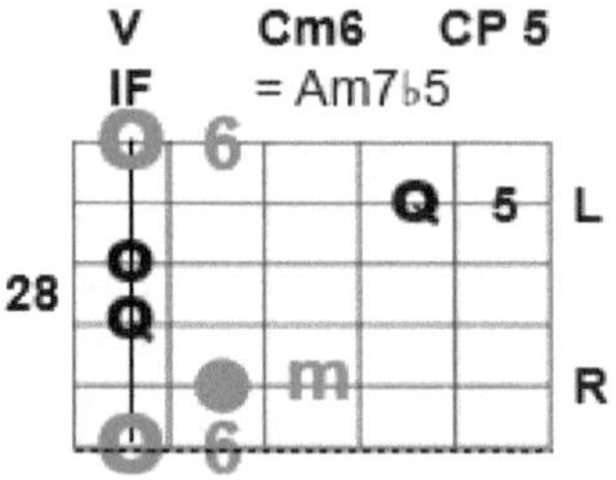

III Cm6 CP 2
IF = Am7♭5

7

I Cm7♭5 = E♭m6
IF CP 3 (?)

figure 17

low E string

III Fm6 CP 4
IF = Dm7♭5

10

III Fm6 CP 4
IF = Dm7♭5

12

V Cm6 = Am7♭5
IF CP 5

16

V Cm6 CP 5
IF = Am7♭5

28

Don't forget, for **C**aug the barré finger must be moved one fret higher and for
Fm in the chord pattern **2** version one fret lower.

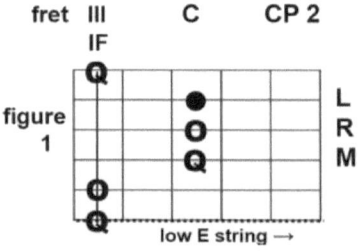

fret III C CP 2
IF

figure 1

low E string →

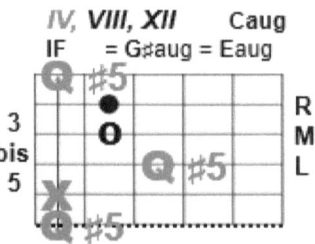

IV, VIII, XII Caug
IF = G♯aug = Eaug

3
bis
5

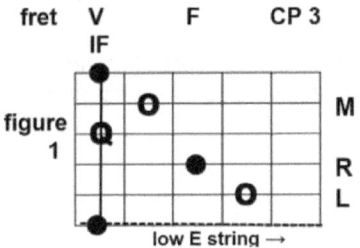

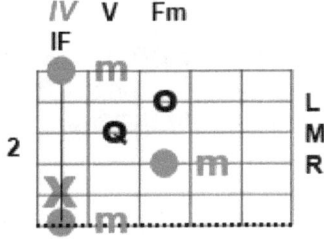

VIII. Rare chords not listed here

You can perhaps try to form them yourself using the 5 chord patterns. If that doesn't work, you can find several companies on the Internet under "Find guitar chords" that may be able to help you.

I have not pursued chords in which, for example, the note **F** occurs in a higher or lower octave in addition to the normal Cmajor chord. Example C11 with the notes C, E, G and **F** in a different octave. It is easy to form if I use chord pattern 1, barré finger on the 8th fret. In chord pattern 2, barré finger on the third fret, I lift the middle finger on the D string and thus produce the new, required note **F** for **C11**.

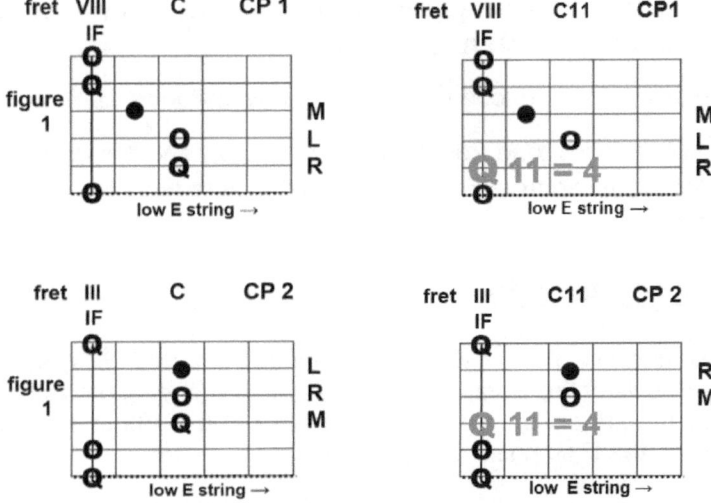

For **Cm11** after **CP 1** I would only have to lift the **m**iddle finger on the **G**-string, for **Cm11** after **CP 2** I would have to move the **r**ing finger on fret number **IV** on the **B** string.

I have created App. **16** for notating new or popular chords. Here you can draw in the chord patterns yourself.

IX. Transposing pieces of music and chords

To get from Cmajor to the first key with only one ♯, I have to call up the **fifth** of the Cmajor scale, i.e. the note **G**. To find the next key with **2 ♯**, I have to look for the fifth again, but in the G major scale. Here, it is the note **D**. This game goes on and on until I reach the key of **C sharp** after **7 ♯**.

For a transposition upwards by a whole tone, therefore 2 (further) ♯ are necessary.

To get from the Cmajor scale to the first scale with a **B♭**, I have to look for the **fourth** of the Cmajor scale, i.e. the fifth that we know by heart, lowered by a whole tone (= 2 half tones); here that would be the tone **F**, i.e. Fmajor. I can easily find the key with **2 ♭** again via the fourth of the Fmajor scale, in this case **B♭ major**. Continue as described above, but always look for the fourth! After **5 ♭** I am in the **D♭ major scale**!

Transposing down a whole tone therefore requires 2 (further) ♭-**flats.**

To move down a whole tone from **G**major to Fmajor, one ♯ is dropped and one ♭ is added. To move from Fmajor to Gmajor, the reverse is true: one ♭ is dropped and one ♯ is added.

X. Another practical tip

It is advisable to apply a dot of white or black paint to frets 3, 5, 7, 9, 15 and 17 on the neck side of the guitar facing the player, depending on whether the neck is made of dark or light wood; use red paint at **fret VIII** to indicate that the note **C** is on the E strings.

Place 2 dots on the **12th** fret to mark the **octave**, then paint over all the dots with clear varnish.

This practice has proved very successful with large, thick acoustic guitars because the player cannot see the markings **on the fingerboard.**

XI. Concluding remarks

Even though I have listed 47 pages DIN A5 for explanations with chord patterns and an additional 18 appendices with figures and fingering charts, finding and forming new chords is much easier than you might think.

You just have to know which notes I produce with the simple major chord with the barré finger and the other 3 fingers on the guitar neck - is it the root/an octave of it, the third or the fifth. See App. 5! Internalize the individual chord patterns!

See also Appendices 17 and 18!

To understand my system for the formation of 1,200 and more barré chords, it is not enough just to study the appendices 11 to 15. Please first read the preface and the text with 47 pages, 113 with tables, explanations and examples. Only then will you be able to understand the relationships between the barré chords!

You only have to deal with **157** barre chords in **5** c hord patterns. That's about **31** per **one** chord pattern. If we assume that approx. **33%** are too high on the guitar neck, you only have to deal with **21** chords per chord pattern, not 1**,200** barre chords **without my system**.

Every guitarist who plays more than just the occasional barré fingering consciously or unconsciously knows at least 3 or 4 notes of the fingered major chord, be it the root, the third or the fifth to the root, even in different octaves, some even know the position of all 6 notes of a major barré chord.

The effort required to know the position of all 6 notes is therefore quite low. Changing a major chord then happens very quickly, sometimes after very little thought.

This is because I can form new chords/derivatives by moving one or more fingers and/or by lifting one or more fingers in **front of the barré finger** in the direction of the bridge.

Once you have played through them, the new fingerings for derivations of simple major or minor chords are easy to remember, as they are structured quite logically. I hope that after reading these lines you will soon only need to check the appendices to be on the safe side.

In addition to the pure major or minor chords, in practice you will usually only find derivations with an additional number or letter such as **C6**. In the best case, only one fingering point in the "table" - see **large** fingering points in **grey or bold black** - needs to be moved, which is usually easy to do. See also **Csus2, Cm, Csus4, C6, C7, CΔ7, Cb9, Cadd9**.

In case of an altered major chord, the alterations are always shown in **large** signs, **large** numbers or the **large** letter **m** in **grey or bold black**. In a diminished seventh chord, for example, only the **root note** or octaves of it may be shown in small black **circles**, because all other notes are lowered by half a tone.

In other commercially available books, a thousand or more black chord patterns are listed in tabular form. Keeping these chord patterns, which you don't understand, in your head is a nonsensical undertaking that can never succeed.

<u>Another simple example for the formation of a new chord according to my method</u>:

I am looking for the not frequently occurring **Csus4** chord after CP **1**.

We know that the sus4 chord only consists of the **3** notes, namely the root, the fourth and the fifth; the third - here note **E** - is replaced by the fourth, the note **E** no longer occurs!

It can be seen from App. 5, that the chord patterns and fingering patterns 1, 2 and 4 only show **one third**, which can easily be replaced by a **fourth**. For the first two chord patterns below, it can be clearly seen that there is only one bold dot as a marker for the third. In chord pattern 1, the finger on the **G** string only needs to be moved forward one fret.

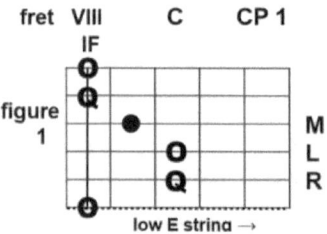
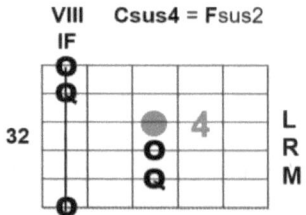

The search with chord pattern **2** is similar, here the finger on the **B** string is moved one fret higher.

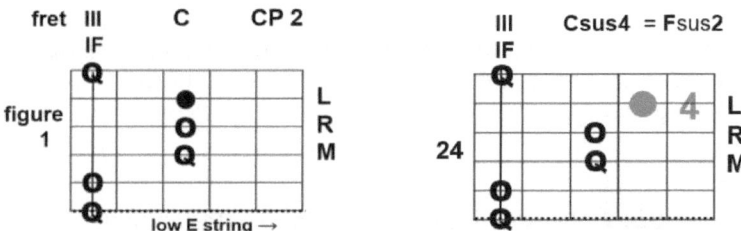

Chord pattern **3** is not suitable for a sus4 chord because the third is played three times here.

There are 4 other possible chord patterns that require a little more thought or are not so common, see App. 11 figure. 32 and 33, App. 12, figure 24 and 25, App. 14, figure 24 and App. 15, figure 20.

How the **sus4 chord** now becomes a **7sus4 chord** by raising just one finger is something I leave to the knowledgeable reader.

A basic note **C** must be changed once to a note 2 semitones lower - in this case **B♭.** Only the notes **C** and **G** and the new notes **F** and **B♭** must be played at least once in the new chord pattern, no other notes are allowed.

But there is more: I can simplify the 4 chord patterns even further by turning a fifth into a fourth - here the **second** note **F** - in all four cases and then raising one finger in front of the barré finger. Solution: see App. 11, figures 32 and 33, and App. 12, figures 26 and 27. However, I prefer the solution with **one** note F because it is easier to deduce and remember.

Appendices 17 and 18 offer further help in the search for unknown chords, because the fingering points for derivations are clearly marked in **large** numbers or the **large** letter **m** in figure **1A** in **grey or bold black**, whereas they are only shown in small letters on the first pages of appendices 11 to 15.

Have fun

Yours, Günter Beyer

XII. Notes

This book also deals with the following chords, which are **missing** in some commercially available overviews and tables of barré fingerings for the percussion guitar:

1. the **Sus2 chords**, there are at least 5 different fingering patterns, 2 of them see down below:

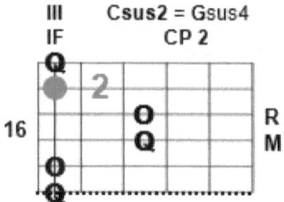 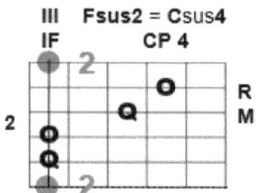

2. the **Add9 chords, i.e.** C9 chords **without seventh**, C9 chords are listed, notes for example: C, E, G and **D** in a different octave, but the chord patterns are often all C7add9 chords. Cadd9 chords exist in at least 6 versions, 2 of them below.

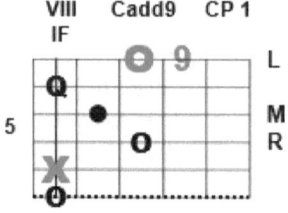 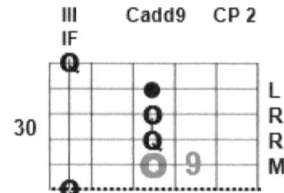

3. The **simple (F) minor chord CP** 4 according to App. 8, figure 2, and App. 14, figure 8.

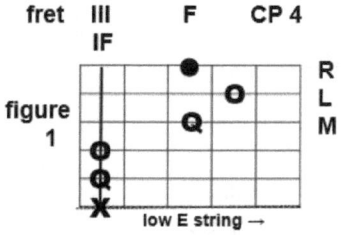 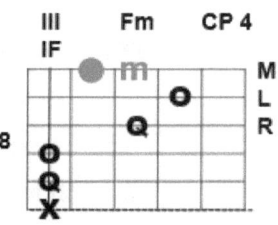

4. the very easy to play C**7 chord with 2 muted strings**, which is not displayed even with "all guitar chords",

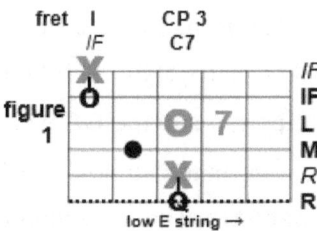

5. the **C7♭9 chord according to App. 9, figure 1**, which is also not listed in "all guitar chords" on the Internet, as I have noticed.

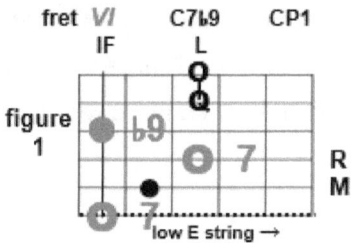

I think the previously (largely?) unknown versions of the chords **C7** and **C7♭9** after points **4.** and **5.** are an enrichment for all guitarists.

I have not carried out any further investigations.

48

XIII. List of Appendices

1 C chords in notes

2 C chords in letters and numbers

3 Piano keyboard for **C** and **F** chords

4 Guitar neck with indication of the notes

5 5+1 Chord patterns for the simple major chord

6 5+1 Chord patterns for the **F**major chord

7 11 Chord patterns of the **C7** chord

8 5 Chord patterns of the simple **minor** chord

9 5 Chord patterns of the **C7♭9** chord

10 Chords with muted strings - 10.1 - 10.2

11 Chord pattern **1** with derivations - 11.1 - 11.3

12 Chord pattern **2** with derivations - 12.1 - 12.2

13 Chord pattern **3** with derivations - 13.1 - 13.2

14 Chord pattern **4** with derivations - 14.1 - 14.2

15 Chord pattern **5** with derivations - 15.1 - 15.2

16 Personal chord patterns for notation

17 Chord pattern **1 + 2** large with derivations

18 Chord pattern **3 - 5** large with derivations

C chords in notes

The name of a chord at the top is the European name if it differs from the English one.

The new notes are large black dots.

C chords in letters and numbers

#	chords	new tones in grey or bold black
1	C	C+E+G
2	$C^{sus2} = G^{sus4}$	C+D+G = G+C+D
3	$Cm = Cmin$	C+E♭+G
4	$C^{sus4} = C^4 = F^{sus2}$	C+F+G = F+G+C
5	$C^{sus2sus4}$	C+D+F+G
6	C^5 = Powerchord	C + G and/or G + C
7	$C^{aug} = C^{5+}$	C+E+G♯
8	$C^6 = Am^7$	C+E+G+A = A+C+E+G
9	C^7	C+E+G+B♭
10	$C^{dim7} = C^{\circ} = C^{verm7}$	C+E♭+G♭+A
11	$C^{7sus4} = C^{7/4}$	C+F+G+B♭
12	$C^{7♭5} = C^{7/5-}$	C+E+G♭+B♭
13	$C^{7♯5} = C^{7/5+}$	C+E+G♯+B♭
14	$C^{7(6)} = C^{7(13)} = C^{7/13}$	C+E+G+B♭+A*)/ *) = 1 octave higher
15	$C^{7add9} = C^{7/9}$	C+E+G+B♭+D
16	$C^{7add9(13)} = C^{7add9(6)} = C^{7/9/13}$	C+E+G+B♭+D+A
17	$C^{maj7} = C^{\Delta7} = C^{7+}$	C+E+G+B
18	$C^{maj7add9} = C^{\Delta7add9} = C^{7+/9}$	C+E+G+B+D
19	$C^{♭9} = C^{9-}$	C+E+G+D♭
20	$C^{add9} = C^9$	C+E+G+D
21	$C^{6add9} = Am^{7(4)} = Am^{7(11)} = C^{6/9} = Am^{7/11}$	C+E+G+A+D
22	$Cm^6 = Am^{7♭5}$	C+E♭+G+A
23	$Cm^{6add9} = Cm^{9/6}$	C+E♭+G+A+D
24	$Cm^7 = E♭^6 = Es^6$	C+E♭+G+B♭
25	$Cm^{7(4)} = Cm^{7(11)} = E♭^{6add9} = Es^{9/6}$	C+E♭+G+B♭+F
26	$Cm^{7♭5} = Cm^{7/5-} = E♭m^6 = Esm^6$	C+E♭+G♭+B♭
27	$Cm^{7(6)} = Cm^{7(13)} = Cm^{7/13}$	C+E♭+G+B♭+A
28	$Cm^{7add9} = Cm^{7/9}$	C+E♭+G+B♭+D
29	$Cm^{7add9(13)} = Cm^{7/9/13}$	C+E♭+G+B♭+D+A
30	$Cm^{7♭9} = Cm^{7/9-}$	C+E♭+G+B♭+D♭
31	$Cm^{maj7} = Cm^{\Delta7} = Cm^{7+}$	C+E♭+G+B
32	$Cm^{maj7add9} = Cm^{\Delta7add9} = Cm^{7+/9}$	C+E♭+G+B+D
33	$Cm^{add9} = Cm^9$	C+E♭+G+D
34	$Cm^{11} = Cm^4$	C+E♭+G+F

The new notes are shown in bold.

C♯ = Cis
A♭ = As

The numbers from 1 to 13 only apply to C chords; for D chords, the numbers start at 1 for D and then increment as in C chords, for example

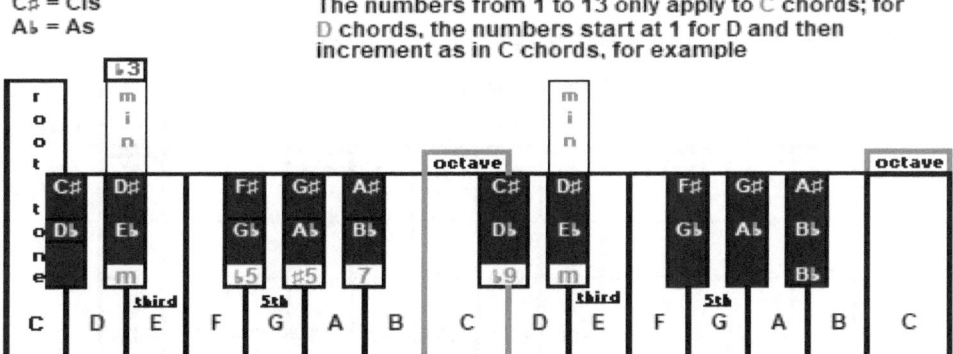

C♯/D♯ etc. = ♯-keys
D♭/E♭ etc. = ♭-keys
C, D, E etc. = name of the tone

The C major chord consists of at least the notes No. 1, 3 and 5 = C, E and G, here outlined in bold. Since the guitar has 6 strings, some notes occur up to 3 times!

The numbers from 1 to 13 are the numbers used here for the shorthand notation of C guitar chords such as C7 = C + E + G + B♭.

Piano Keyboard   F chords

F♯ = Fis
A♭ = As

The numbers from 1 to 13 only apply to F chords, for G chords, the numbers start at 1 for G and then increment as in F chords, for example

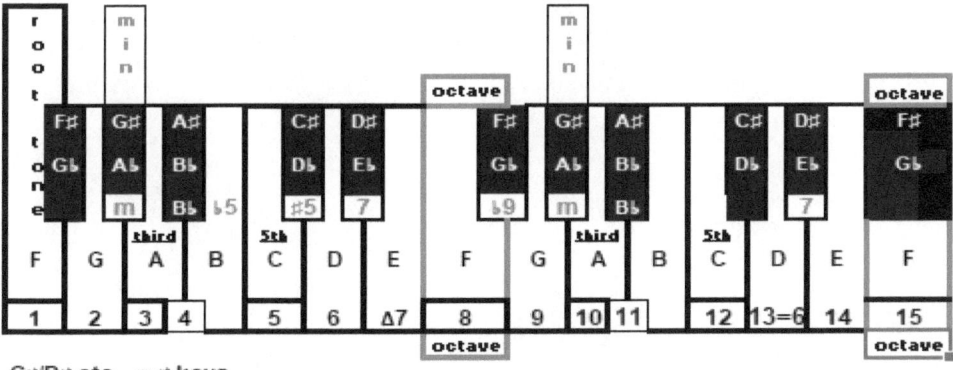

C♯/D♯ etc. = ♯ keys
D♭/E♭ etc. = ♭ keys
F, G, A etc. = name of the tone

The F major chord consists of at least the notes No. 1, 3 and 5 = F, A and C, here outlined in bold. Since the guitar has 6 strings, some notes occur up to 3 times!

The numbers from 1 to 13 are the numbers used here for the shorthand notation of F guitar chords such as F7 = F + A + C + E♭.

Neck of the Guitar

For the sake of simplicity all tones are capitalized

Fret number

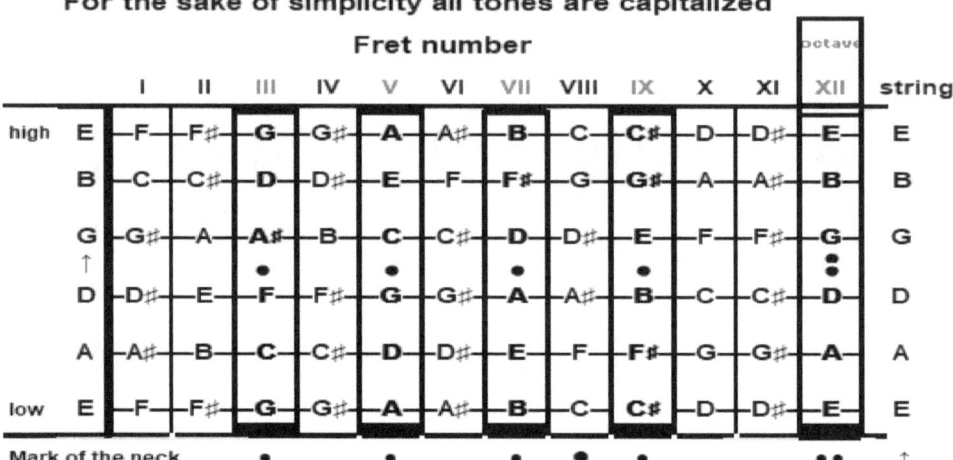

		I	II	III	IV	V	VI	VII	VIII	IX	X	XI	XII	string
high	E	F	F♯	G	G♯	A	A♯	B	C	C♯	D	D♯	E	E
	B	C	C♯	D	D♯	E	F	F♯	G	G♯	A	A♯	B	B
	G	G♯	A	A♯	B	C	C♯	D	D♯	E	F	F♯	G	G
	D	D♯	E	F	F♯	G	G♯	A	A♯	B	C	C♯	D	D
	A	A♯	B	C	C♯	D	D♯	E	F	F♯	G	G♯	A	A
low	E	F	F♯	G	G♯	A	A♯	B	C	C♯	D	D♯	E	E

Mark of the neck

The frets No. **III, V, VII, IX** and following are mostly market with white or black dots on the neck or provided with a large ribbon of mother-of-perlmutt. Two points on the neck means octave. On the E string lies again the tone E, but one octave higher.

For solos from fret XIII and higher the tones lies as at the frets I to VIII, but one octave higher.

Changes opposite to the root chord = **large** $\mathbf{O}$ **o** = root tone/octave
Arabic number = number of the fret   ●   ● = third to lower root ton
m = minor = ♭3 = little third   **Q**   **Q** = 5th "   "   "   "
CP = chord pattern   **X**   **x** = muted string, do not
                                                   strike the string

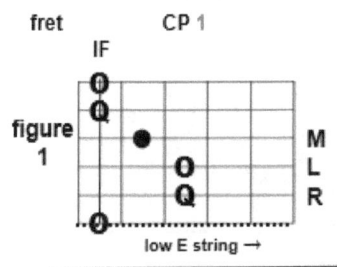

Fingering for chords
IF = index finger
M = middle finger
R = ring finger
L = little finger
grip points connected
with vertical line(s)
= barre finger(s)

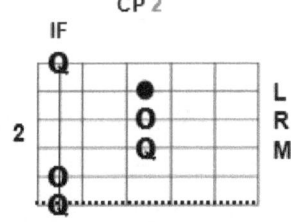

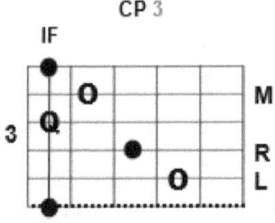

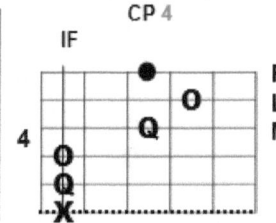

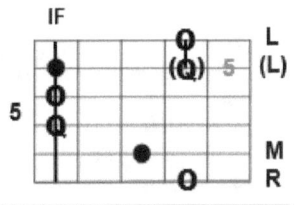

Chord pattern **1**   The fundamental note or the 2nd octave of it lies on the E strings. It appears 3 times. With the barre finger on fret 1 this results in an F chord, on fret III in the G and on fret VIII in the C chord. The third is present once so that the minor and sus4 chords can be easily formed. The chords and derivatives of CP 1 and 2 are usually only spread over 3 frets.

Chord pattern **2**   The fifth is on the E strings, the fundamental occurs twice. With the barre finger on fret 1 this produces the B♭ major chord, on fret III the C chord and on fret VIII the F chord. The third is only present once, so that the sus2, the minor and the sus4 chords are easily formed.

Chord pattern **3**   The third is on the E strings and occurs three times. With the barre finger on fret 1 this results in the D flat major chord, on fret III in the E flat chord and on fret V in the F chord. For the minor chord, the barre finger must be pushed back one fret towards the saddle. See App. 13, CP 3, Figure 2.

The chords and derivatives of fingering patterns 3 to 5 are usually distributed over 4 frets.

Chord pattern **4**   The low E string must be muted or must not be struck. The third on the high E string lies two frets higher than the barre finger. With the barre finger on fret 1 this results in the E flat chord, and on fret III in the F chord. The third only occurs once.

Chord pattern **5**   The root note or the 2nd octave of it occurs 3 times. With the little finger on the high E-string and the ring finger on the low string - same fret - the fundamental or the 2nd octave of it is produced on the E-strings, the barre finger is 3 frets below the fingering points on the E-strings. The third occurs twice. A 2nd variation with 2 fifth is shown in brackets, the little finger must be bent backwards on the B string so that the fifth sounds on the B string and the fundamental on the high E string.

5+1 Chord pattern of the Fmaj chord

Changes opposite to the root chord = **large** 🔘   O = root tone/octave
Arabic number = number of the fret   ● ● = third to lower root ton
m = minor = b3 = little third   Q Q = 5th " " " "
CP = chord pattern   X X = muted string, do not
strike the string

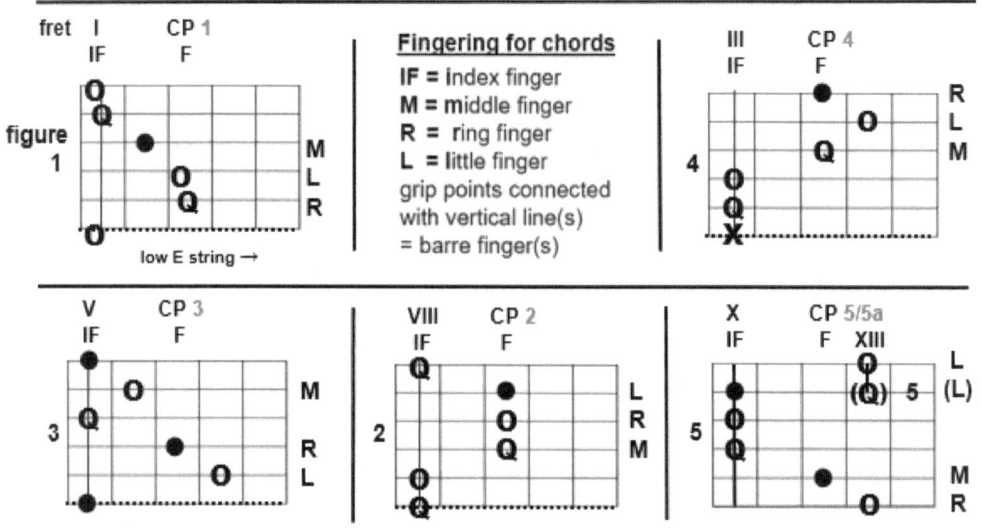

Fingering for chords
IF = index finger
M = middle finger
R = ring finger
L = little finger
grip points connected
with vertical line(s)
= barre finger(s)

Note the order of the tones in the individual chord patterns from bottom to top! Also note the order of the chord patterns on the guitar neck in ascending order – 1, 4, 3, 2 and 5!

CP 1 = **root tone**, 5th, **root tone**, third, 5th, **root tone**
CP 2 = 5th, **root tone**, 5th, **root tone**, third, 5th
CP 3 = third, **root tone**, third, 5th, **root tone**, third
CP 4 = muted string, 5th, **root tone**, 5th, **root tone**, third
CP 5 = **root tone** , third, 5th, **root tone**, third (5th), **root tone**

Every major chord can be fingered according to the 5 chord patterns, with version 5a there are even 6 variations. However, it should be noted that there are usually 2 to 3 chords with the fingering patterns that are too high on the guitar neck, so they are generally not used, but they are there.

The F chord after CP 5 will only used as a final chord, if at all.

The grip pattern 5a is as follows:

Instead of placing the little finger on the high E-string on fret XIII, place the little finger on the B-string on fret XIII and bend it backwards so that the note C, i.e. the fifth of the F major chord, is created on the B string and the root note F is produced on the high E string as in CP 5.

11 Chord fingerings of the chord C7

grey or bold black underlined
= notice and remember the chords

Changes opposite to the root chord = **large** ⬤ o = root tone/octave

Arabic number = number of the fret   ⬤ ● = third to lower root ton

m = **minor** = **♭3** = **little third**   **Q** Q = 5th "   "   "   "

CP = **c**hord pattern   **X** X = muted string, do not strike the string

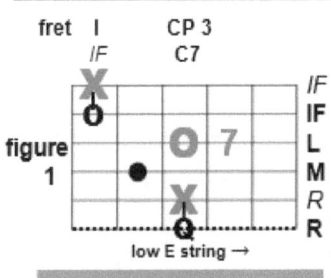

figure 1

Fingering for chord**S**

IF = **i**ndex **f**inger
M = **m**iddle finger
R = **r**ing finger
L = **l**ittle finger
grip points connected
with vertical line(s)
= barre finger(s)

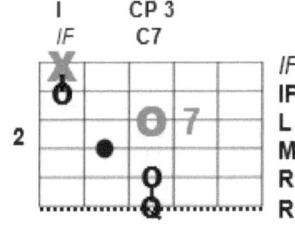

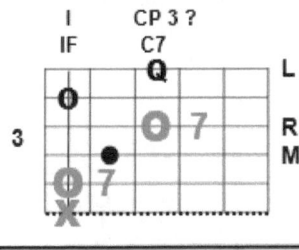

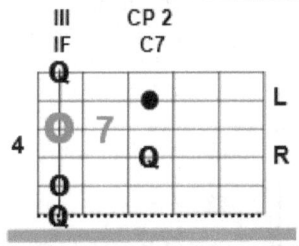

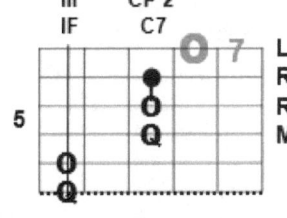

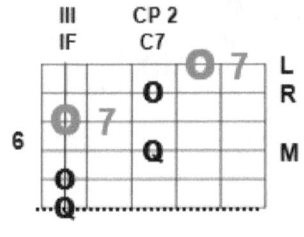

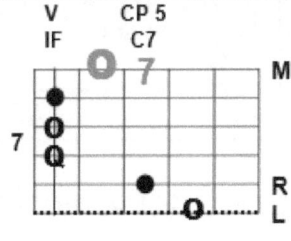

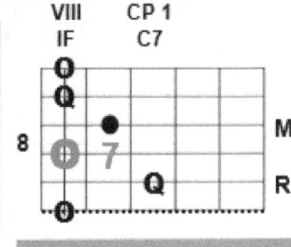

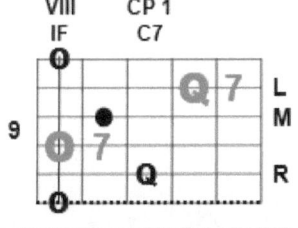

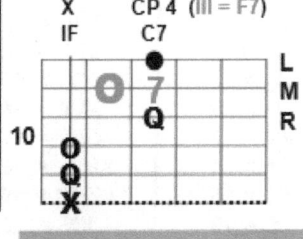

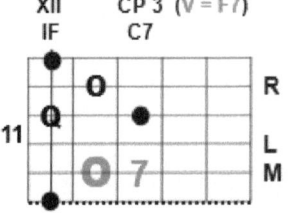

grey or black underlined
= notice and remember fingering pattern

Changes opposite to the root chord = large O = root tone/octave
Arabic number = number of the fret ● = third to lower root ton
m = minor = b3 = little third Q = 5th " " " "
CP = chord pattern X = muted string, do not
strike the string

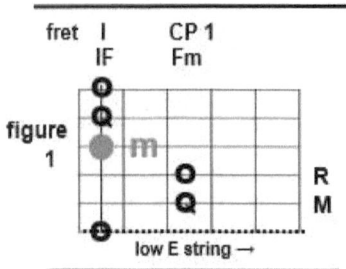

fret I   CP 1
IF   Fm
figure 1
R
M
low E string →

Fingering for chordS
IF = index finger
M = middle finger
R = ring finger
L = little finger
grip points connected
with vertical line(s)
= barre finger(s)

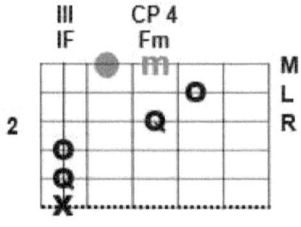

III   CP 4
IF   Fm
2
M
L
R

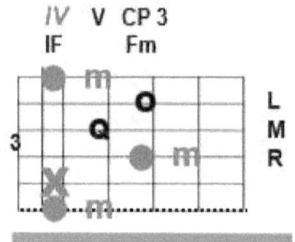

IV V CP 3
IF   Fm
3
L
M
R

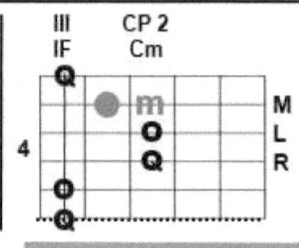

III   CP 2
IF   Cm
4
M
L
R

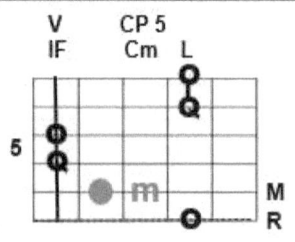

V   CP 5
IF   Cm   L
5
M
R

Refresher for Roman numerals

I = 1		XI = 11	
II = 2		XII = 12	
III = 3		XIII = 13	
IV = 4		XIV = 14	
V = 5		XV = 15	
VI = 6		XVI = 16	
VII = 7		XVII = 17	
VIII = 8		XVIII = 18	
IX = 9		XIX = 19	
X = 10		XX = 20	

5 Chord fingerings of the C7♭9 chord

Changes opposite to the root chord = **large** O o = root tone/octave

Arabic number = number of the fret ● = third to lower root ton

m = minor = ♭3 = little third Q q = 5th " " " "

CP = chord pattern X x = muted string, do not strike the string

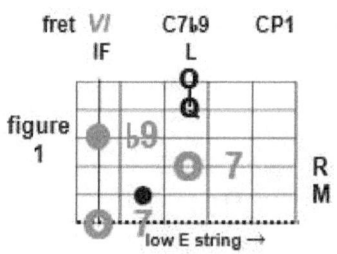

Fingering for chordS
IF = index finger
M = middle finger
R = ring finger
L = little finger
grip points connected
with vertical line(s)
= barre finger(s)

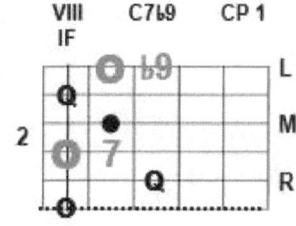

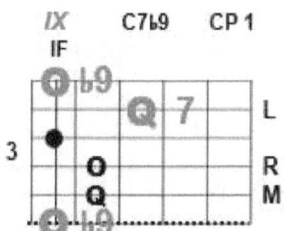

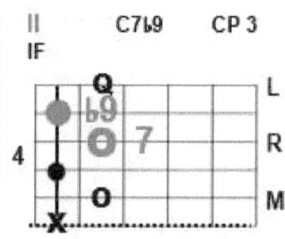

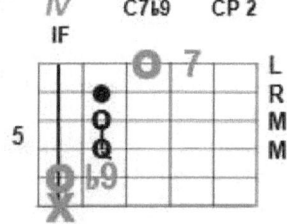

The chords C7♭9 are sorted by:

Figure 1: root tone lies on the high E string = C
Figure 2: ♭9 lies on the high E string = D flat
Figure 3: ♭9 lies on the high E string = D flat
Figure 4: fifth lies on the high E string = G
Figure 5: Seventh lies on the high E string = B♭

so that the search and the movement are easy to understand.

I think that with the solution shown in figure 1 I have found a new way to create a 7♭9 chord that can also be played easily and over all 6 strings. This new variant is not found in chord finders on the Internet or not listed in a book with 1,200 chords.

The chord can be found as follows:
1. Finger the C chord, CP 1, with barre finger on the VIIIth fret. The note C is therefore on the high E string.
2. Now go down 2 frets - fret VI - and then finger the corresponding **dim7** chord , in this case the B♭dim7 chord.
3. Bend the little finger on the B string backwards so that it sounds the new note C, the missing fundamental note, on the high E string.

Changes opposite to the root chord = **large**   **O**   o = root tone/octave

Arabic number = number of the fret   ●   ● = third to lower root ton

m = minor = ♭3 = little third   **Q**   Q = 5th " " " "

CP = chord **p**attern   **X**   X = muted string, do not strike the string

---

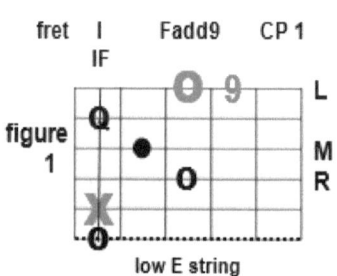

Fingering for chords

IF = index finger
M = middle finger
R = ring finger
L = little finger
grip points connected
with vertical line(s)
= barre finger(s)

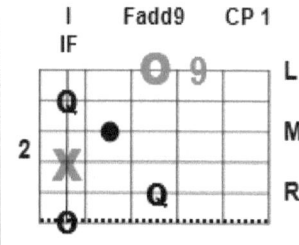

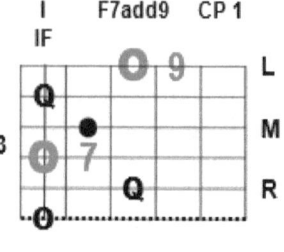

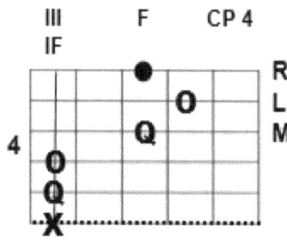

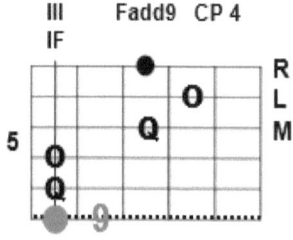

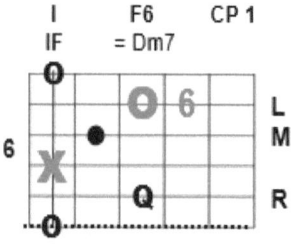

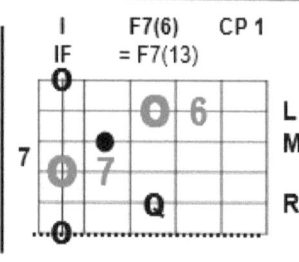

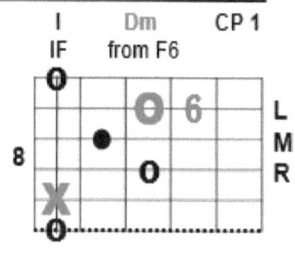

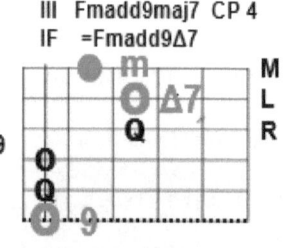

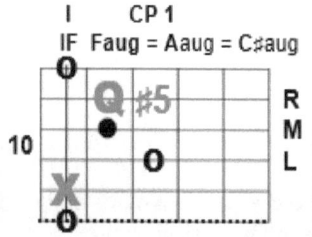

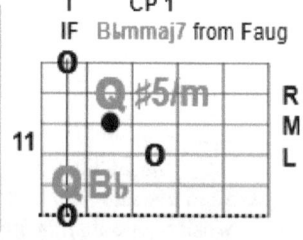

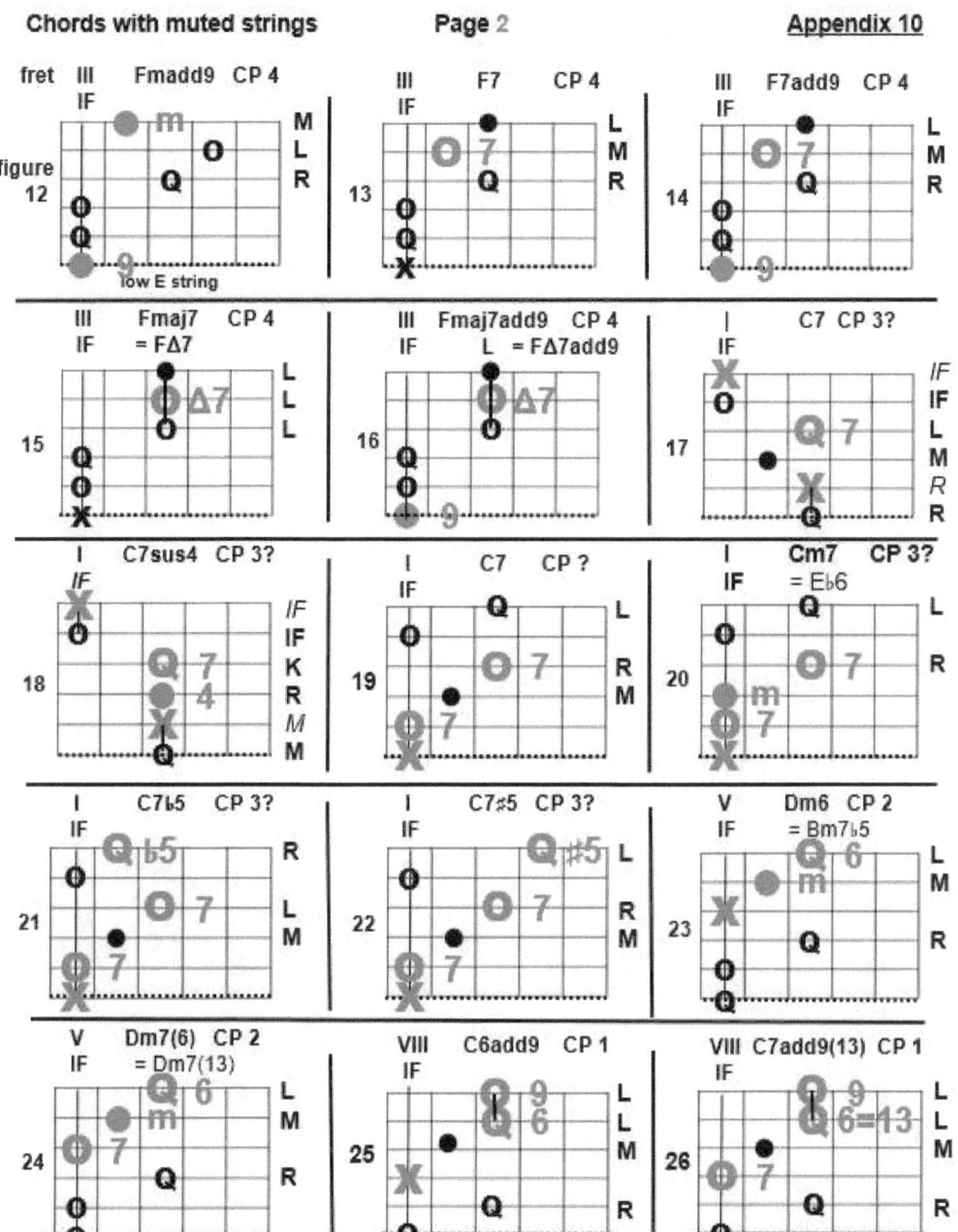

Explorations

For fingering patterns 17 and 18, the index finger and ring finger must be bent slightly backwards to dampen both the high E string and the A string; for fingering patterns 25 and 26, the little finger must be used as the 2nd barre finger to produce the 9th note on the high E string and the 6th note on the B string.

Chord pattern 1 with derivations

Appendix 11

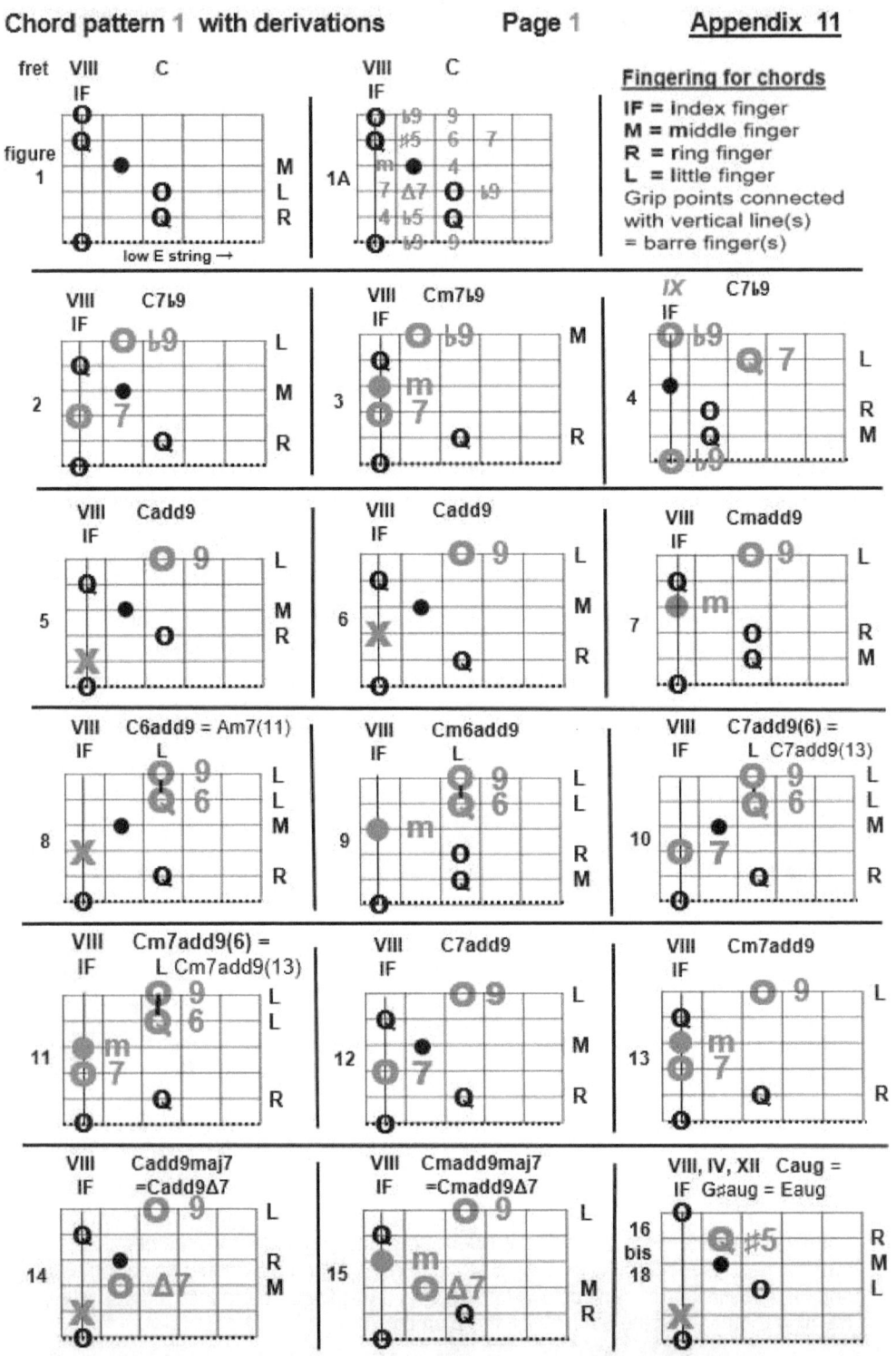

Fingering for chords

IF = **i**ndex finger
M = **m**iddle finger
R = **r**ing finger
L = **l**ittle finger
Grip points connected
with vertical line(s)
= barre finger(s)

Chord pattern 1 with derivations   Page 2   Appendix 11

fret VIII   C6 = Am7

figure 19

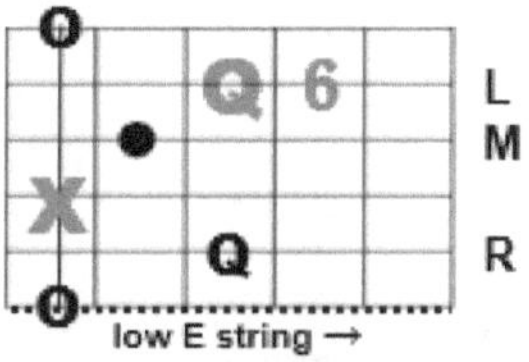

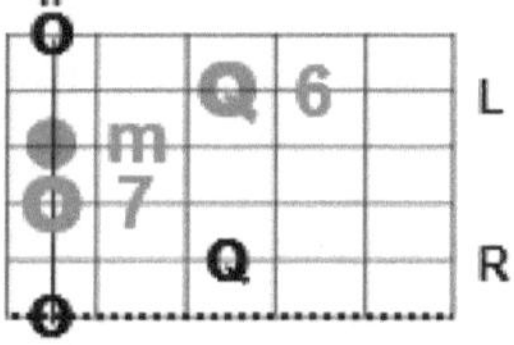

low E string →

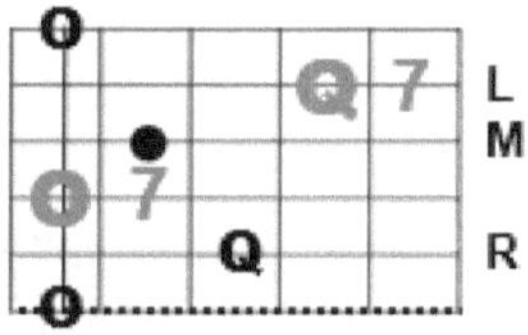

VIII   Cm6 = Am7♭5

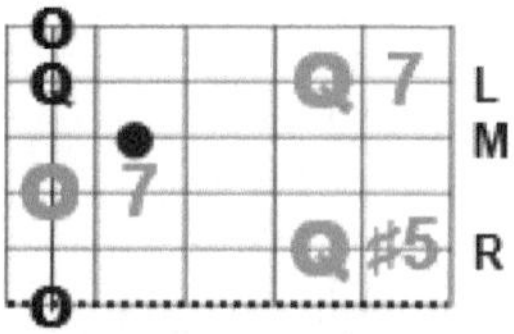

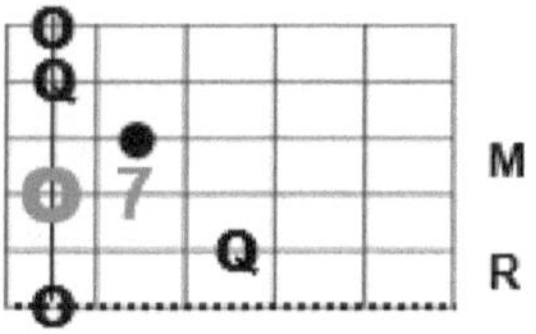

20

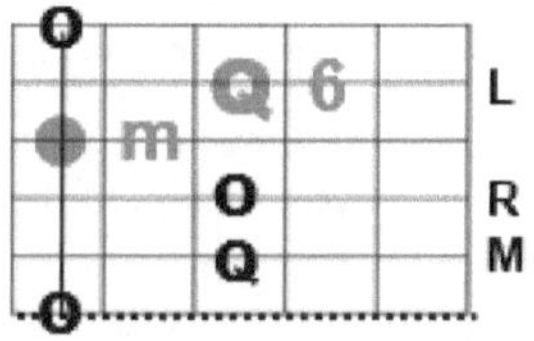

VIII   C7(6) = C7(13)

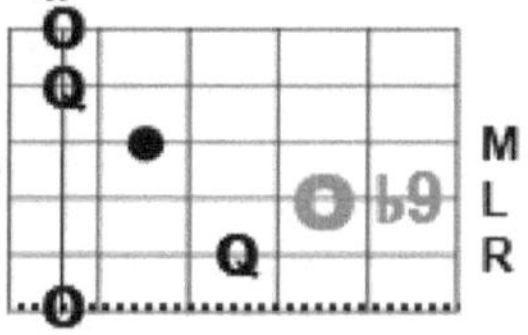

21

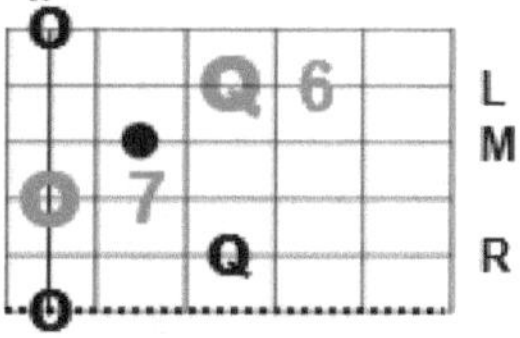

22   Cm7(6)

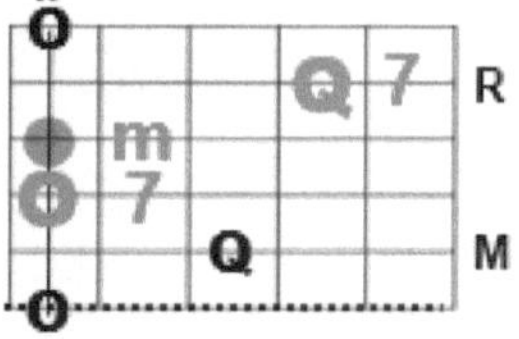

23   C7

24   C7#5

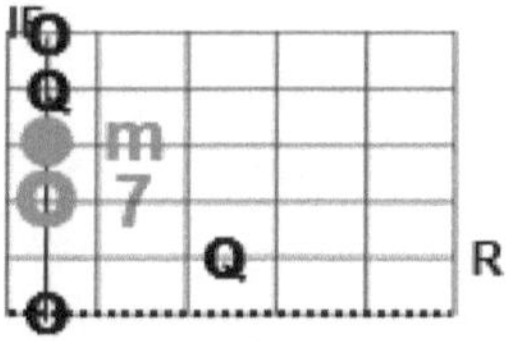

25   C7

26   C♭9

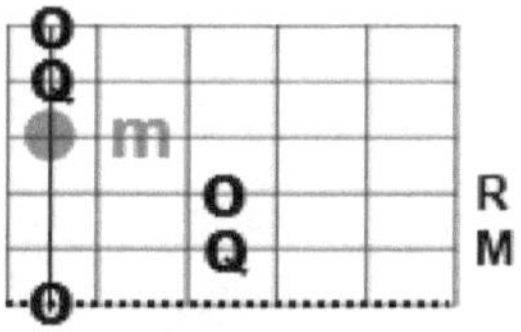

27   Cm7 = E♭6

28   Cm7 = E♭6

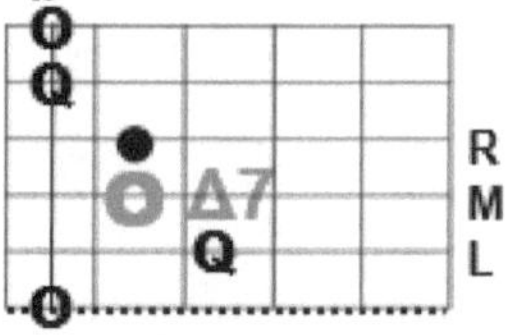

29   Cm

30   XI   E♭maj7 = E♭Δ7

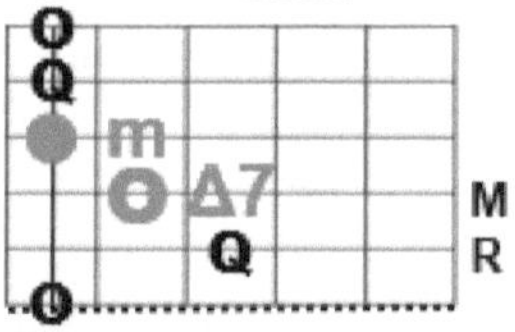

31   Cmmaj7 = CmΔ7

32   Csus4 = Fsus2

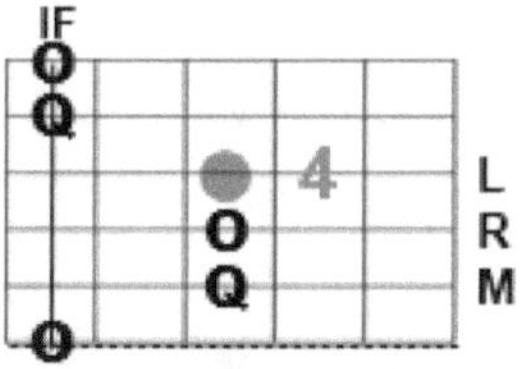

33   Csus4 = Fsus2

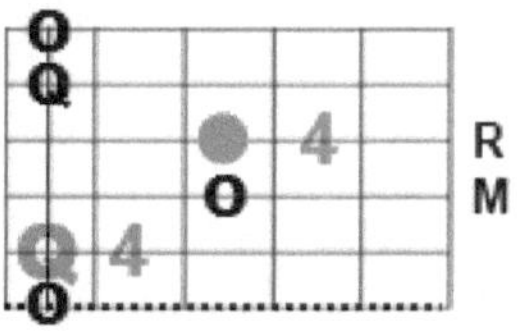

34   C7sus4

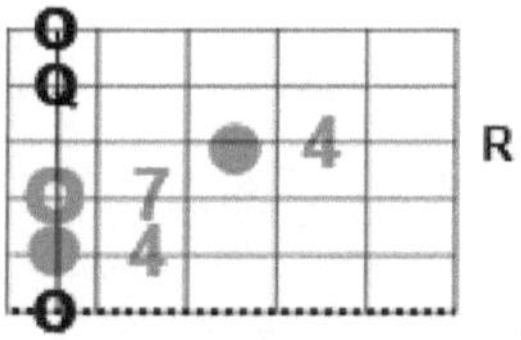

35 bis 38   VIII, II, V, XI C° = Cdim7 = G♭° = A° = E♭°

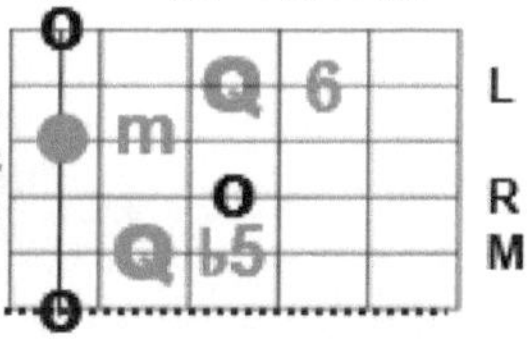

39   VI   C7♭9

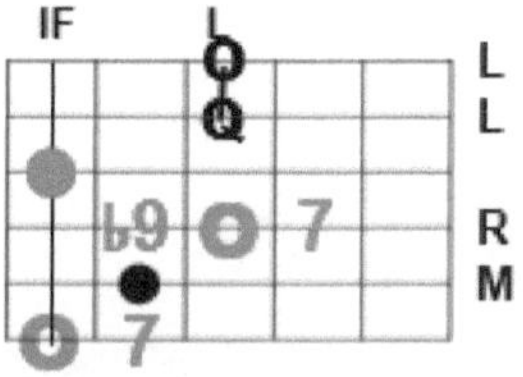

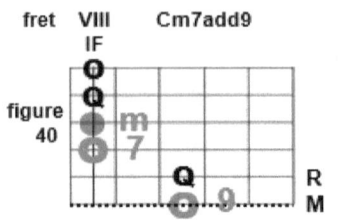

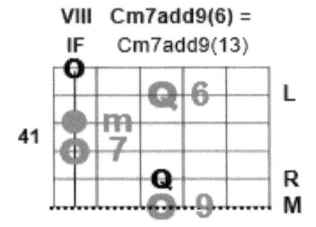

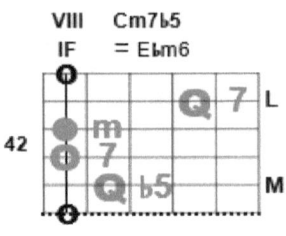

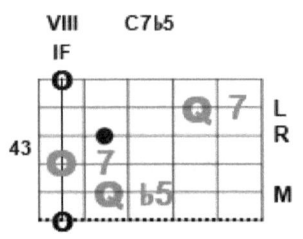

The figfures 42 and 43 were added later.

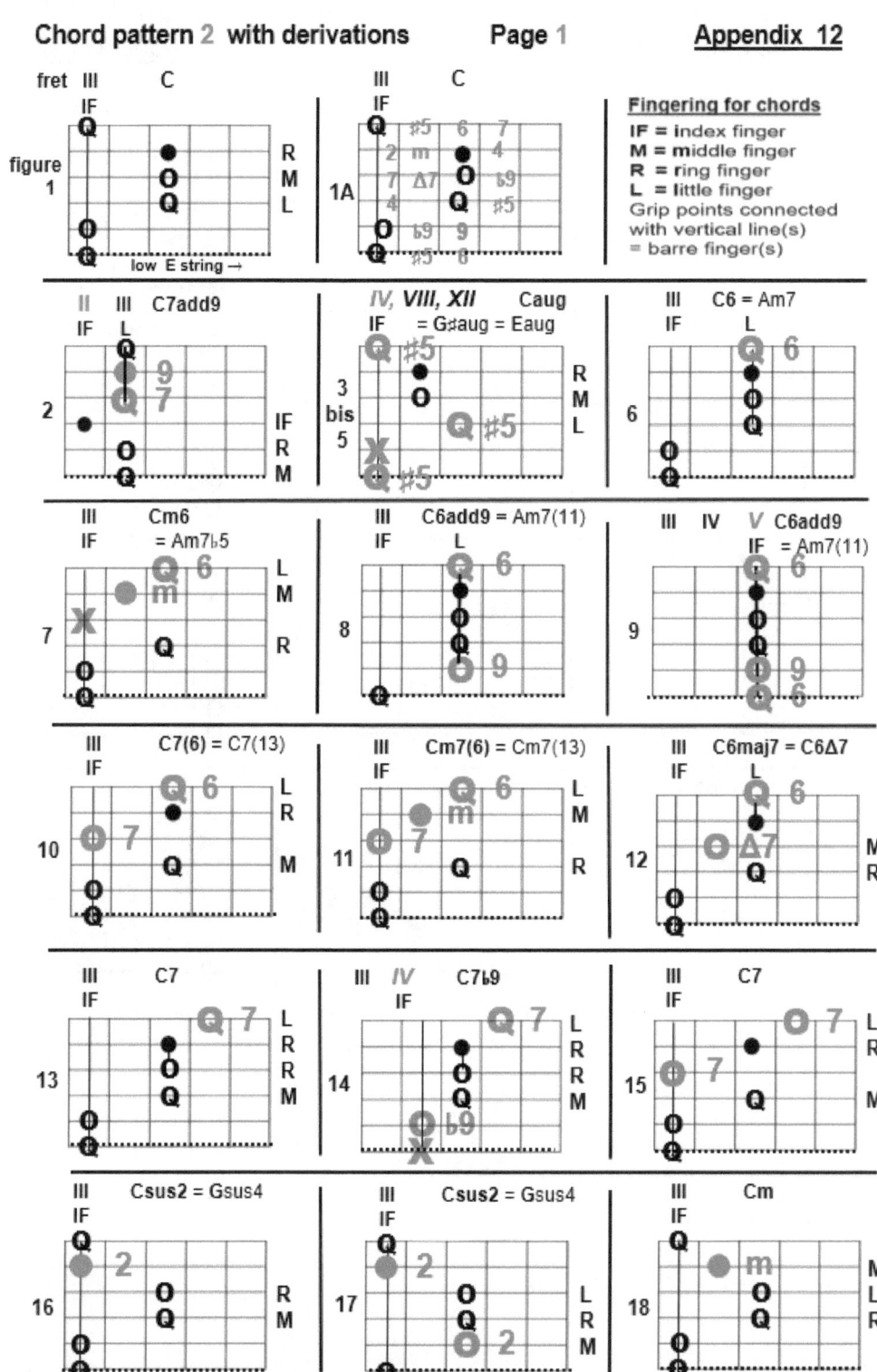

Chord pattern 2 with derivations   Page 1   Appendix 12

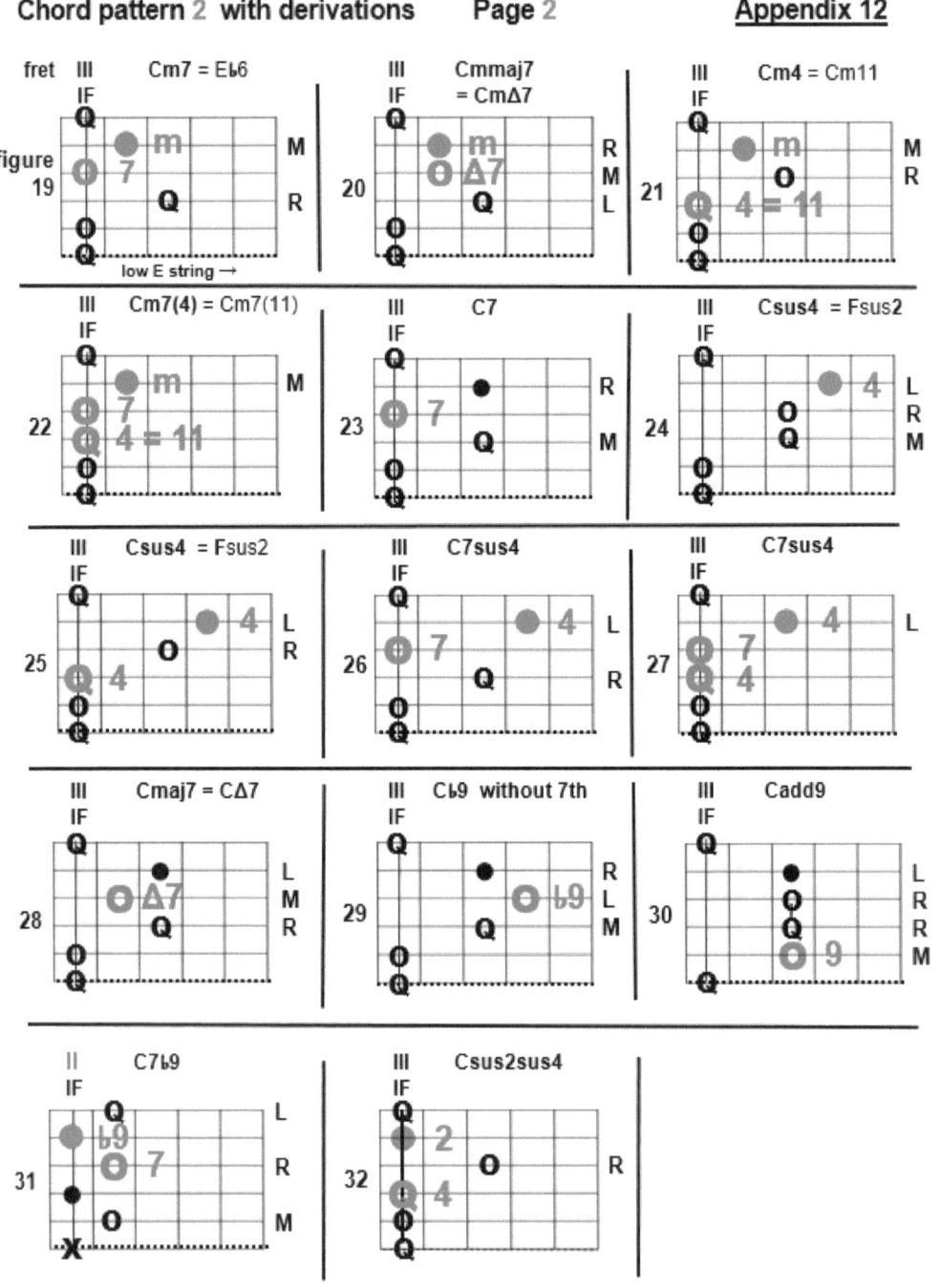

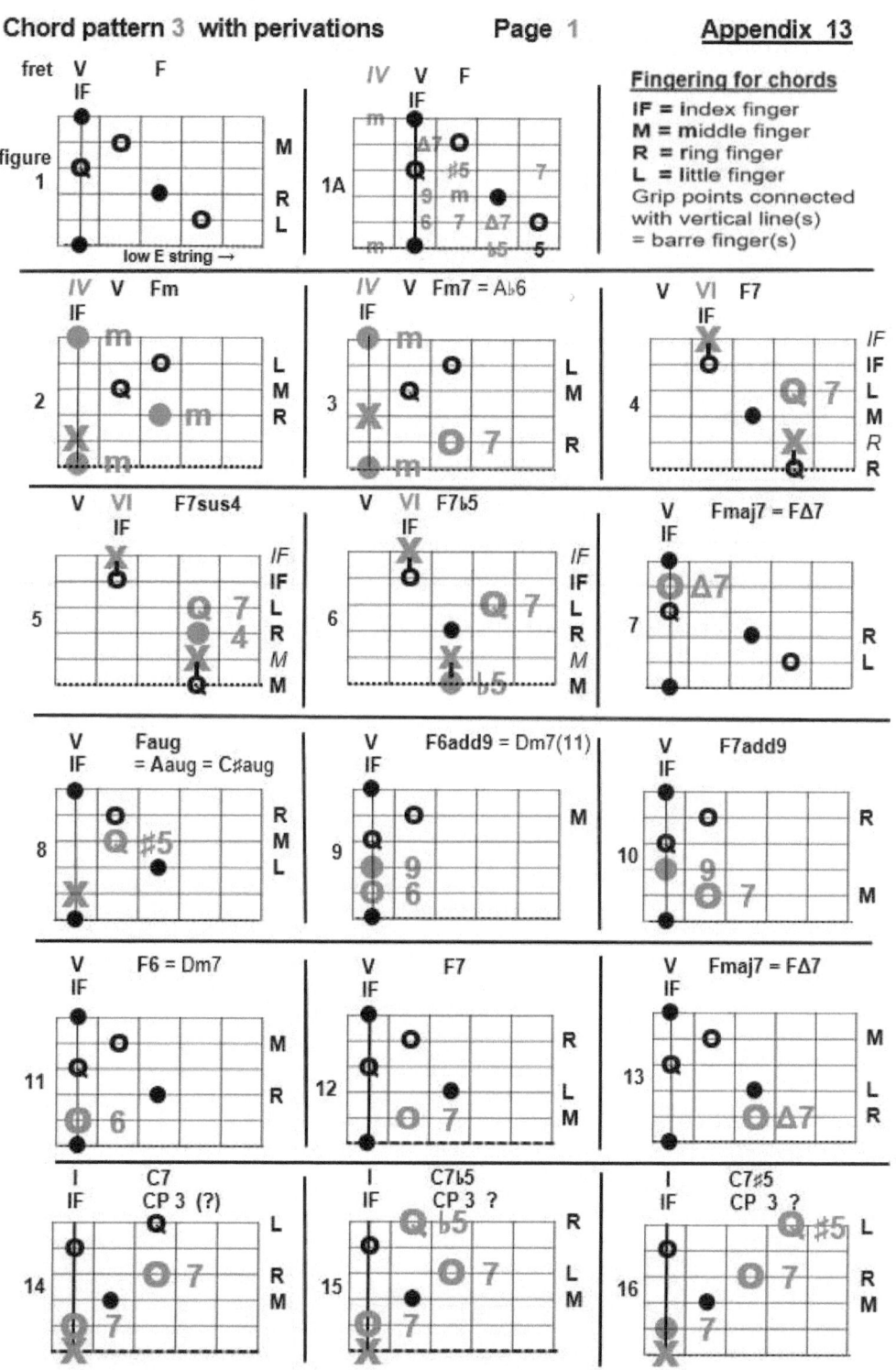

Chord pattern 3 with perivations   Page 1   Appendix 13

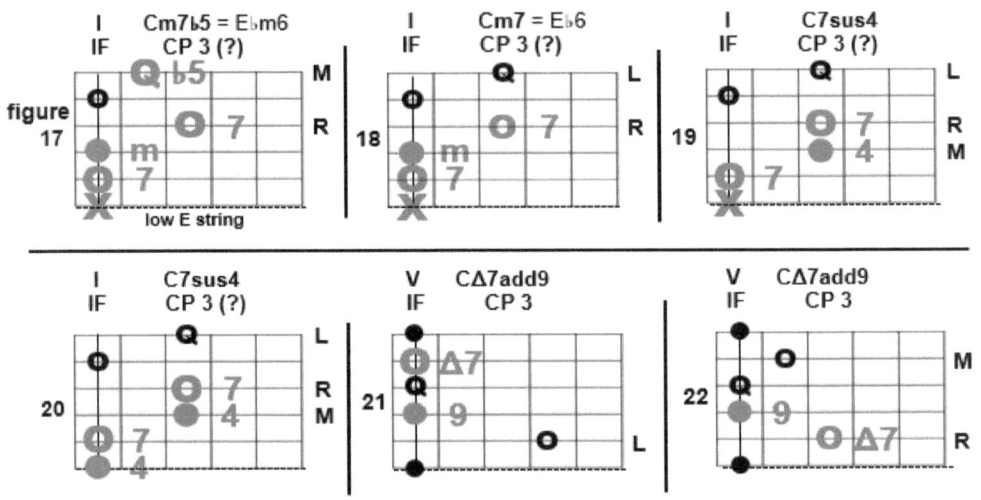

The figures number 21 and 22 were added later.

Chord pattern 4 with derivations   Page 1   Appendix 14

Fingering for chords

IF = **i**ndex finger
M = **m**iddle finger
R = **r**ing finger
L = **l**ittle finger
Grip points connected with vertical line(s) = barre finger(s)

Figure 1 — III / IF — F — R L M — low E string →

Figure 1A — III / IF — F

Figure 2 — III / IF — Fsus2 = Csus4 — R M M

Figure 3 — III / IF — F6add9 = Dm7(11) — L R

Figure 4 — III / IF — Fm6add9 — R M

Figure 5 — III / IF — Fm6add9 — L R M

Figure 6 — III / IF — F7add9 — M R L

Figure 7 — III / IF — Fadd9maj7 = Fadd9Δ7 — L R M

Figure 8 — III / IF — Fm — M L R

Figure 9 — III / IF — Fmadd9 — M L R

Figure 10 — III / IF — Fm6 = Dm7b5 — M R

Figure 11 — III / IF — Fm6add9 — M R

Figure 12 — III / IF — Fm6 = Dm7b5 — R L M

Figure 13 — III / IF — Fm7 = Ab6 — R M L

Figure 14 — III / IF — F6 = Dm7 — L R

Figure 15 — III / IF — F6add9 — L R

Figure 16 — III / IF — F7 — L M R

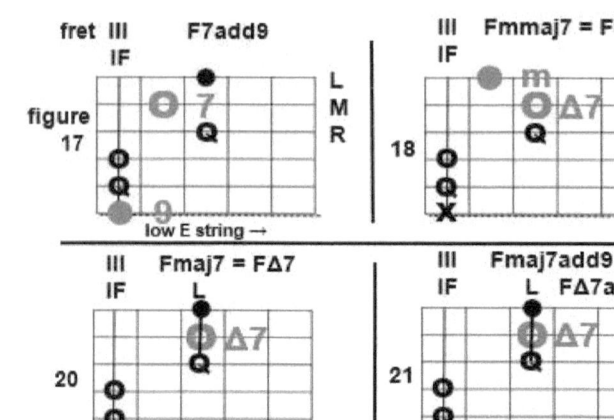

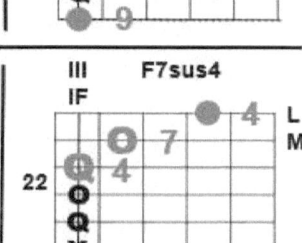

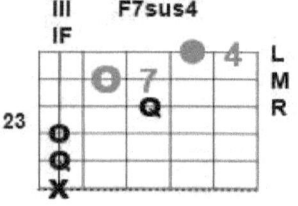

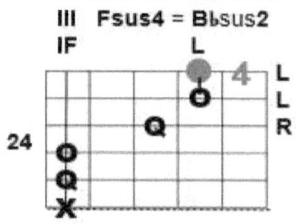

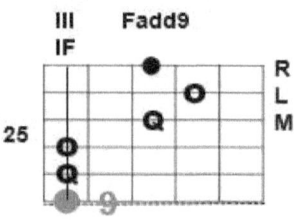

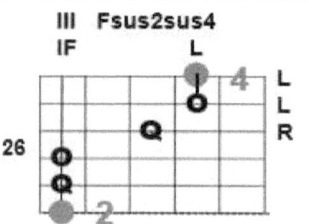

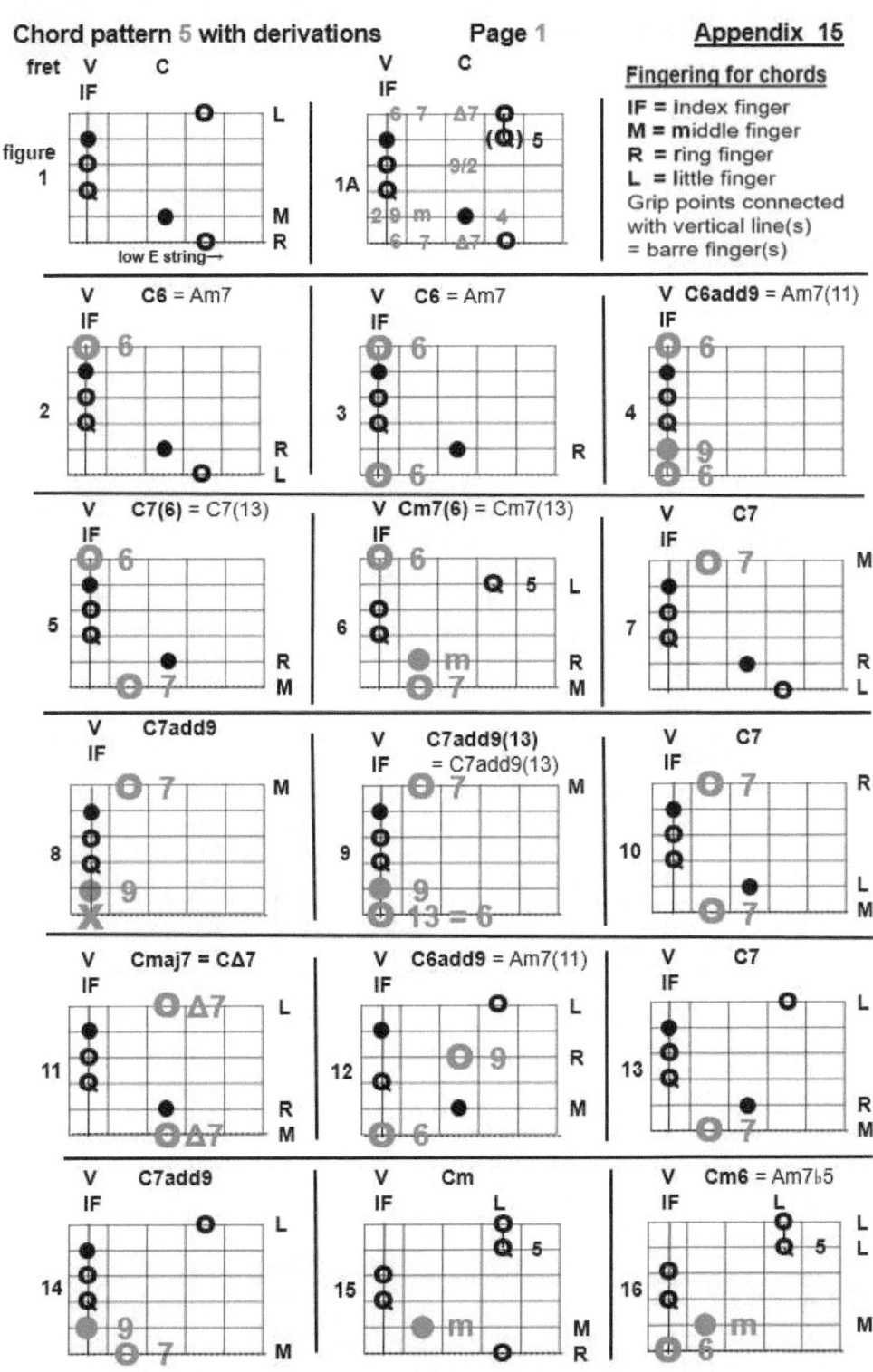

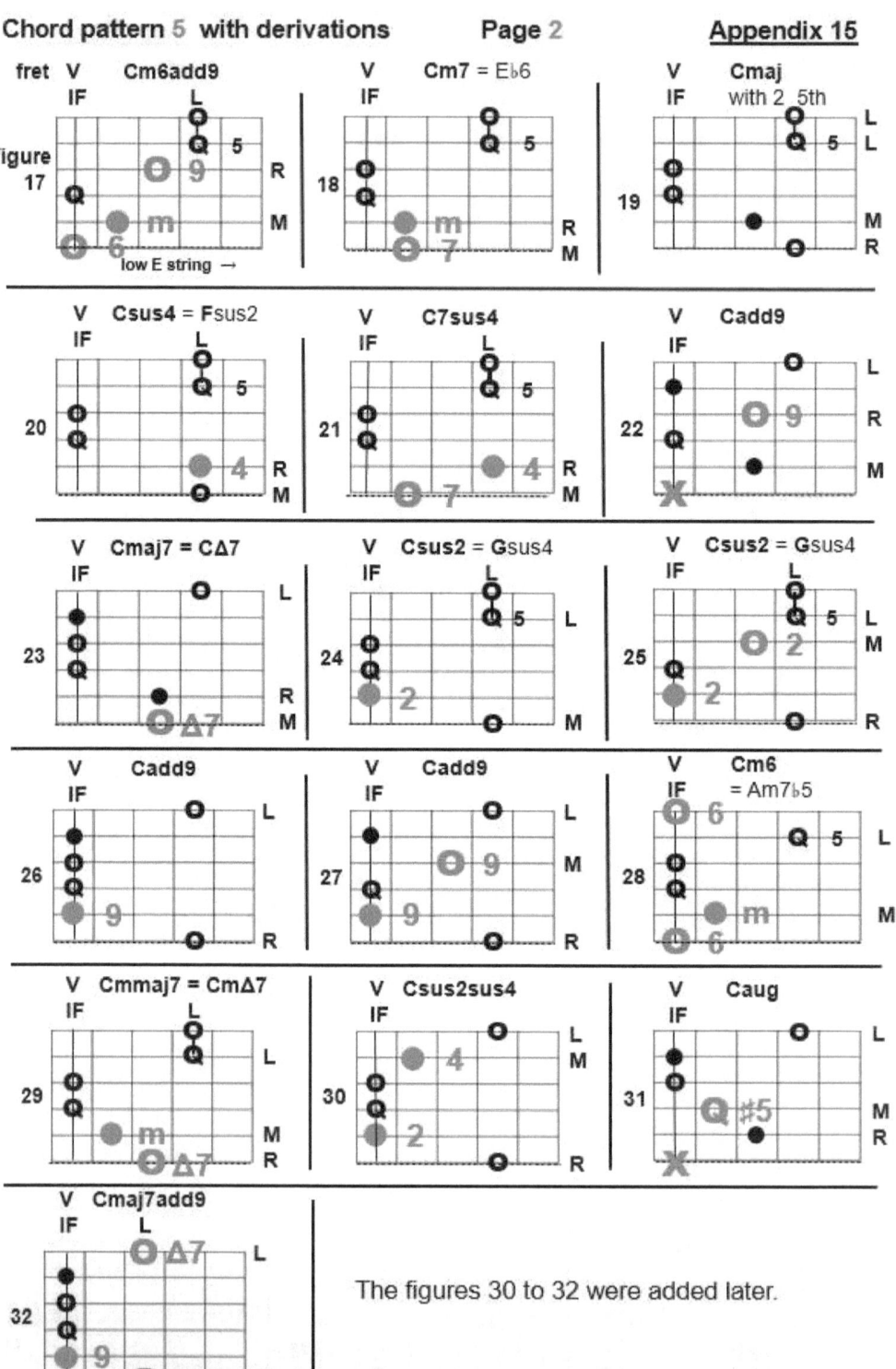

Chord pattern 5 with derivations Page 2 <u>Appendix 15</u>

The figures 30 to 32 were added later.

Personal chord fingerings for notice   Appendix 16

Changes opposite to the root chord = **large** 🔘   o = root tone/octave
Arabic number = number of the fret   ● = third to lower root ton
m = minor = ♭3 = little third   Q = 5th "   "   "   "
CP = chord pattern   X = muted string, do not
                                                strike the string

fret

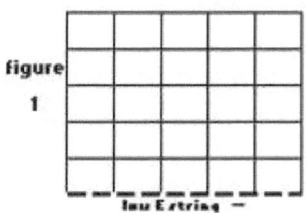

figure
1

Fingering for chords
IF = index finger
M = middle finger
R = ring finger
L = little finger
Grip points connected
with vertical line(s)
= barre finger(s)

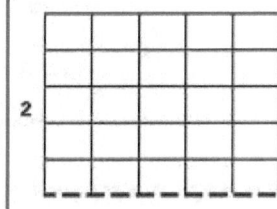

2

fret

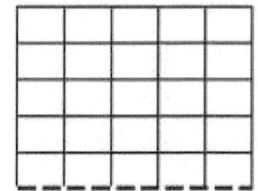

3

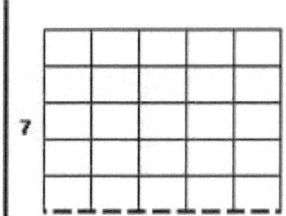

4

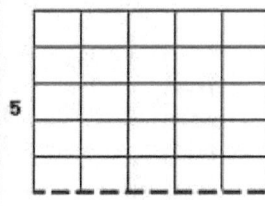

5

fret

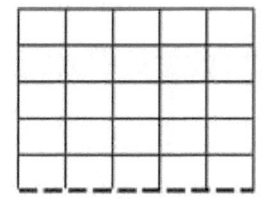

6

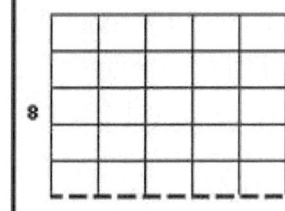

7

8

fret

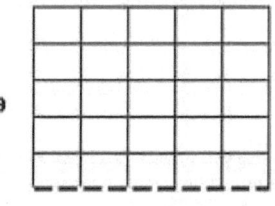

9

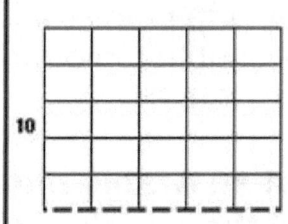

10

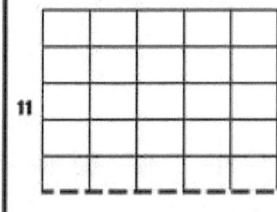

11

Chord pattern **1** with derivations

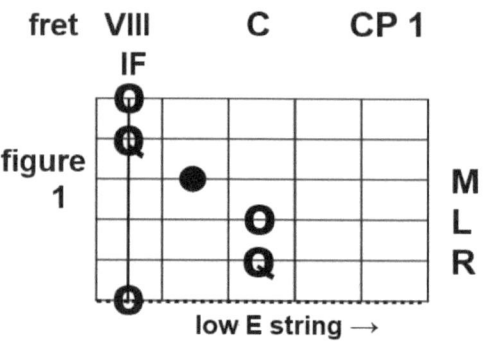

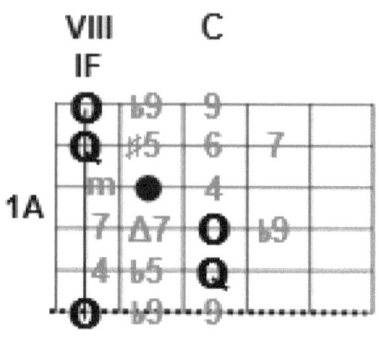

Chord pattern **2** with derivations

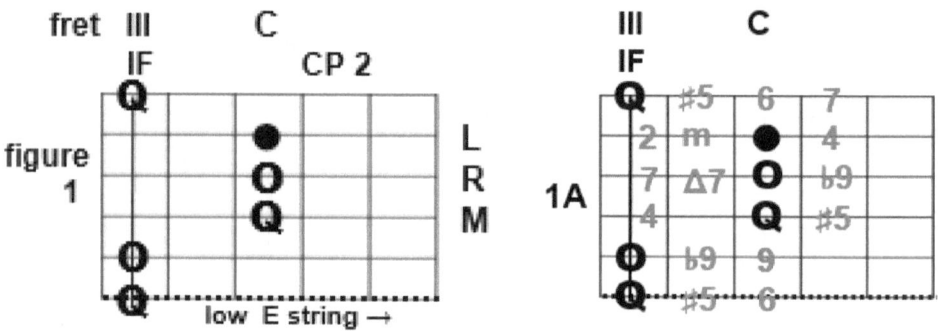

App. 17 and 18

The numbers or the letter **m** for minor show the exact grip point for new chords /derivations

App. 7 to 15

The significantly **larger** fingering points and to the right the larger number(s) or the letter **m** for minor in **grey or bold black** show the grip points of new, possible chords or derivations of the simple major chord.

Grip points without an Arabic number or the letter m always are parts of the simple major chord.

Chord patterrn 3 with derivations

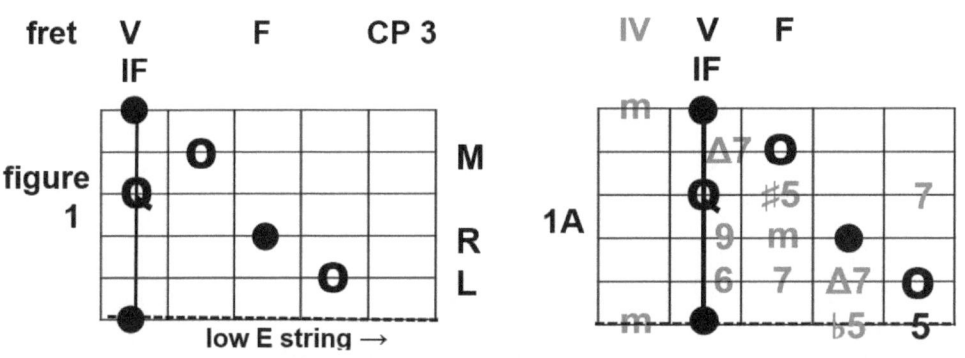

Chord pattern 4 with derivations

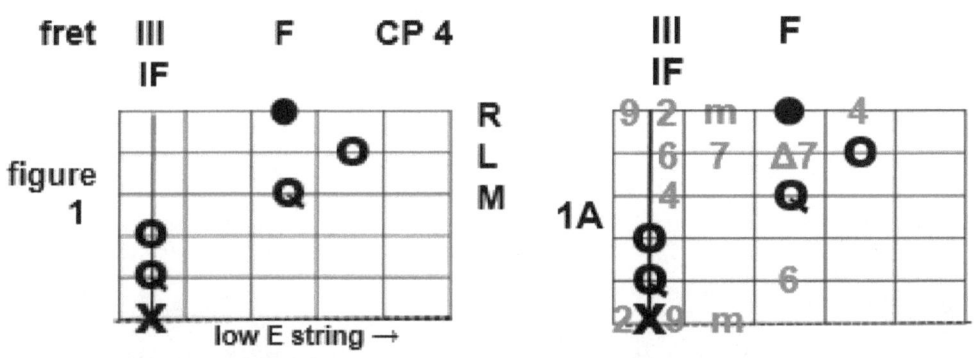

Chord pattern 5 with derivations

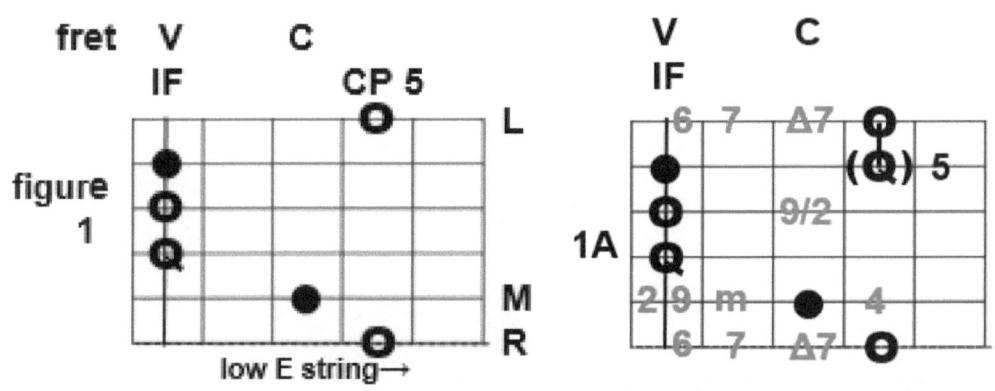

Zeitfracht Medien GmbH
Ferdinand-Jühlke-Straße 7
99095 Erfurt, Deutschland
produktsicherheit@kolibri360.de